Prayer
That Gets Answers

Prayer That Gets Answers

Learning the secrets of effective prayer

Living Word Series
Book I

Colin Dye

New Wine Press

New Wine Ministries
PO Box 17
Chichester
West Sussex
United Kingdom
PO19 2AW

ISBN 978-1-905991-51-8

Typeset by **documen**, www.documen.co.uk
Cover design by CCD, www.ccdgroup.co.uk
Printed in the United Kingdom

CONTENTS

1 God Answers Prayer

People often turn to prayer as a "last resort" in times of trouble or great need. They believe that to pray is about all you can do when there is nothing else to be done. For others, prayer is a like a placebo pill – they're not really sure it achieves anything, but it serves the purpose of making them feel better. Authentic prayer is nothing like either of these worldly views. It is not something we should turn to when "all else" has failed. Neither is it a pointless religious exercise that just makes people feel better. It is, in fact, a dynamic spiritual encounter between a human being and the Living God – an encounter which has transformed the lives of countless individuals throughout history. Prayer changes the lives of those who engage with it. Prayer can even alter the course of nations. Real prayer has far-reaching consequences.

As believers, prayer is far more than an activity we occasionally participate in. It must be central to our whole way of life. Why do we pray? Why do people pray in general? We pray because we need to find answers to the situations and circumstances that arise in our lives. We need answers that really work, not the empty consolation of praying without any real knowledge of who we are praying to, as mentioned earlier. We all have needs relating to our lives as individuals and we want to know whether God will hear and answer us.

Many Christians know in theory that they have a loving Heavenly Father who longs to meet their needs, but they often find it hard to express this truth with much confidence when it comes to praying. The purpose of this book is to help those who have doubts, and to remind us all that God wants us to learn to pray firstly with the absolute certainty that He hears us, and secondly with the assurance that He wants to bless us abundantly.

If you knew for sure that God's heart was to bless and prosper you, more abundantly than you could imagine, what would you pray for?

Whilst it is many other things besides, the Bible is a book that reflects God's character and reveals His heart towards us. It shows us exactly what He is like in His nature and it gives us an insight into how He operates. One thing that comes through in Scripture very clearly is what God does for people who seek Him with their whole heart, with every fibre of their being: *He meets with them.* Read the following promises from the Bible:

"You will seek me and find me when you seek me with all your heart."   (Jeremiah 29:13, NIV)

"Those who know your name will trust in you, for you, LORD, have never forsaken those who seek you."
(Psalm 9:10, NIV)

"The lions may grow weak and hungry, but those who seek the LORD lack no good thing."
(Psalm 34:10, NIV)

"Blessed are they who keep his statutes and seek him with all their heart." (Psalm 119:2, NIV)

"I love those who love me, and those who seek me find me." (Proverbs 8:17, NIV)

"The LORD is good to those whose hope is in him, to the one who seeks him."
(Lamentations 3:25, NIV)

"For everyone who asks receives; he who seeks finds; and to him who knocks, the door will be opened."
(Matthew 7:8, NIV)

Psalm 145:18 says,

"The LORD is near to all who call upon Him, to all who call upon Him in truth."

This means that God is nearer to us than we may have ever imagined. When God says He is "near" to us, He means He is closer to us than the very air we breathe. It should be a huge source of comfort to us to know that God is only one prayer away from us, all the time.

In the book of Acts, the apostle Paul, referring to God, said,

"In Him we live and move and have our being"
(Acts 17:28)

What Paul wanted to convey here, bearing in mind that his audience was a group of people who worshipped many gods and saw them as distant, impersonal beings, is that God – the holy, all-powerful, almighty One – is with us every second of every day. Rather than being distant and indifferent, God is concerned with our everyday needs, whether they be basic physical needs or the deep concerns of our heart.

Whatever the need we have or whatever is on our mind, God is already listening and waiting for us to speak to Him about it. Even before we can fully articulate our prayer to Him, He is aware of our need and is patiently waiting for us to ask Him for help. God has promised in Scripture that He will answer those who call earnestly and sincerely on Him. Since it is completely impossible for God to lie to us or to be unfaithful to His Word, we can be *absolutely certain* that He will respond to us. God answers sincere prayer. He will not fail to answer us when we call.

God's hearing and answering of our prayers does not depend on our performance or our "qualifications", as we would view them. God has no favourites. We are all His "favourite". His love and attention is focused upon all those who call on Him in simple faith.

Scripture is unequivocal about the fact that when we pray, God will answer us *every time*, and yet, there are some "conditions" we must consider if we want our prayers to be powerful and not just hollow words.

Prayer plus ...

In Scripture prayer is never found working in isolation. Prayer always has a catalyst – some factor which activates and empowers it. In other words, prayer in the Bible is always *mixed* with something else. Prayer (simply speaking out words to God) on its own is never enough to get answers from God. If you read about prayer in the Bible you will see that in order for it to be effective, it always takes place in a certain context with specific criteria attached to it.

Once we learn how to mix our prayer with the things that activate it, our prayer life will be transformed. Instead of being dull and lifeless, our praying will be exciting and energising; it will literally come alive!

What are the catalysts that cause our prayer life to be lifted to a new level? In Scripture we see prayer combined with a number of other factors. For example ...

◊ Prayer is mixed with God's will and God's Word

◊ Prayer is mixed with faith and action

◊ Prayer is mixed with praise and thanksgiving

◊ Prayer is mixed with fasting and persistence

Our prayer life will become dynamic as we learn how to combine our praying with some or all of these ingredients, as well as others that the Holy Spirit will reveal to us in the Word as we engage with Him. We discover, as we begin to put it into practice, that prayer really does work when combined with these things. But if there is one essential ingredient to prayer that we cannot do without it is this: *confidence!* If we don't have the confidence to approach God, believing that He wants to answer us, then we will be defeated even before we begin.

Many Bible teachers say that God only ever answers prayers in one of three ways: He either says, "Yes", "No" or "Wait". On the surface, this sounds a very plausible, even biblical, argument, but there is a problem with it. Often people will say this because it offers a very convenient get-out clause. If your prayer gets answered, then God must have said, "Yes." If clearly it doesn't, then He must have said, "No." If nothing happens, then I guess God is telling you to wait! To me this is often a front to cover up our unbelief. It is an excuse that allows us to opt out of really engaging with God and persisting in prayer.

Before any reader begins to feel that I am over-simplifying the matter, let me say this: God is sovereign and prayer is a divine mystery! Nothing I write in this book can alter that fact, but I do believe that God has revealed much in Scripture about prayer and how we are to engage with Him through it. It is true that despite having done "everything" they can to the best of their knowledge, some people still do not see the answers to their prayers. There is no comfortable answer to this, and I don't pretend that there is. But I do know that God has called us to boldly engage in prayer and that nothing supernatural will happen in our lives without it.

Another excuse people use to justify "unanswered prayer" in their lives is by insisting all prayer should begin or end with, "If it be your will". In the next chapter we shall see that God wants us to pray "according to His will" and not take the lazy way out of praying, "If it be your will". This form or prayer should only be used when, having searched the Scriptures and waited on God, we still do not have a complete understanding of what God has for us in a certain situation. Only at these times is it right to pray "If it be your will". But in most situations God's will is clearly revealed in Scripture and by the Spirit's testimony to our hearts. This confident knowledge of His will and intentions is at the heart of prayer that gets answers from God.

Praying with confidence

At times, any Christian, regardless of whether they work in an office, factory, or whether they are a pastor leading a church, can grow cold in their faith. It may be because of discouragement, fear, disappointment or a host of other reasons, but when this happens people often stop praying. When this happens, we cease to interact with God in a meaningful way, which means that we don't hear Him as well as we did, and frequently we turn to human reasoning to try to figure out the problems in our life. It is quite ironic that in the times when we most need to pray, we tend to stop praying and try to work things out for ourselves, but that is what human beings are prone to do.

Many wrong ideas, however, stem from people who have lost their confidence in God's Word. Once we hang up the lifeline of prayer and disconnect from God we are increasingly influenced by human thoughts and opinions – what the Bible refers to as "worldly wisdom" – a code for living that appears to make some sense superficially, but often contravenes the godly wisdom that would guide our lives effectively. We must learn to avoid this subtle trap and settle the matter in our minds once and for all: God will never answer prayers that originate from human reasoning or ideas. God answers prayers that are prayed in accordance with His will.

"This is the confidence we have in Him, that if we ask anything according to His will, He hears us. And if we know that He hears us, whatever we ask, we know that we have the petitions that we have asked of Him."
(1 John 5:14-15)

Read this verse again and meditate on it for a while. Let your spirit absorb it and dwell on it. Know in your heart that we can be 100% confident that God will answer our prayers when we approach Him and pray according to His will, as revealed in the Bible. God shows us clearly in His Word what His will for us is, so we can approach Him confidently and with joy. It thrills the heart of God when we come to Him expecting a positive answer.

God always says "Yes!"

The Bible knows nothing of "Yes ... No ... Wait" teaching. In Scripture the equation of prayer is very simple: we look into God's will, we pray according to His will, and we receive the answer to our prayers. Prayer does not have to be as complicated as we often make it.

We know that the Bible reveals God's will to us. We know that we have been given access to the presence of God by His Spirit. And we know that the blood of Jesus gives us assurance in the presence of an awesome and holy God. In addition to these things, we need to know that there is a smile on the Father's face when we come to Him and pray with confidence according to His will. God's answers are always "Yes" in Jesus.

> *"For the promises of God in Him are 'Yes', and in Him 'Amen', to the glory of God through us."*
> (2 Corinthians 1:20)

Have you noticed that when children ask their parents for something, and the mother or father doesn't really want to give an answer there and then, they will say things like, "We'll see" or "Maybe later" in order to be non-committal? In many ways this is just a subtle way of saying "No", but they don't want to eliminate all hope of an answer and disappoint their child! God is not like this. We don't serve a "We'll see" kind of God. We don't serve a God who is reluctant to grant our requests or who has to be pleaded with and persuaded. Instead He likes to shout a loud "Yes!" in response to our prayers.

The Apostle Paul explains why to us in the verse above: God says "Yes" to us because He has already said yes to His Son. God has granted His Son all the resources of His kingdom – and we are in His Son, in Christ. God's "Yes" to Jesus echoes throughout the universe for all eternity for anyone who will hear it and respond in faith.

Summary:

◊ Authentic prayer is a dynamic spiritual encounter with God, not an empty religious exercise. Prayer must be central to our life as a believer.

◊ We should not be hesitant about coming to God with our needs. He already knows what our needs are, but it is an expression of our reliance upon Him that we come to Him and ask for them to be met.

◊ In the Bible, prayer is combined with many other "catalytic" factors in order to be truly effective, but the one factor we cannot do without is confidence. We need to align ourselves with the truth that God is willing to grant our requests so we should be confident in asking Him.

◊ We don't need to beg or plead with God when bringing our needs to Him, because He delights in answering the prayers of His children, prayed in accordance with His will.

2 *Praying with God's Will*

In the same way that it would be pointless to set off on a trip to visit someone without knowing their address, we need to know God's correct "address" in order to visit Him in prayer. We won't receive answers to our prayers unless they go to the right place!

The right place is found in Jesus. The Bible tells us that all the promises of God are delivered to us in Christ. In Jesus is where we find the answers to all our prayers. In Jesus is where we receive the yes from God we are searching for. The promises of God are exclusive to Jesus, the carrier of all God's blessings. Jesus is our Saviour, Healer, Deliverer, Friend, Lord and Provider.

Praying in Jesus' Name

In the previous chapter we mentioned some of the ingredients that can be combined with prayer in order to make it potent and effective, the most important of these being *confidence* – having an expectancy that God desires to answer us and bless us.

The reason for and source of our confidence comes from Jesus. Scripture makes it clear that we are to pray *in Jesus' name* and that when we do so, we should expect an answer. When we pray on our own behalf, out of our own initiative, it achieves little, if anything. But Scripture promises us that when we request something in Jesus' name, then,

> *"Whatever you ask in My name, that I will do, that the Father may be glorified in the Son."*
>
> (John 14:13)

Jesus Himself promised this to us, His followers. When we pray in His name He promises to do *whatever we ask* according to His will. His precious, life-giving name is the key to our prayers being answered. This truth is so important that Jesus reiterated the promise to His disciples immediately,

> *"If you ask anything in My name, I will do it."*
>
> (John 14:14)

There can be no room for doubt. But just in case we are still not fully convinced of Jesus' promise, He restates it *again ...*

> *"Most assuredly, I say to you, whatever you ask the Father in My name He will give you."*
>
> (John 16:23)

... and again!

> *"Until now you have asked nothing in My name. Ask, and you will receive, that your joy may be full."*
>
> (John 16:24)

The message is clear: God will answer *all* your prayers – in Jesus' name. There are no half measures and no refusals.

This is God's heart towards prayer and the correct biblical understanding about prayer.

Praying with God's will

At times we become so familiar in our prayers that we forget we are engaging in a powerful spiritual activity and not simply a human one. It is a dynamic spiritual interaction. Prayer is the method by which God operates and activates His will. This is why God requires that prayer must be made in Jesus' name.

In order for our prayers to be effective in Jesus' name, *we must line up perfectly with the will of God*. This is precisely what Jesus did. Jesus is the perfect expression of the Father's will, and that is why all the authority of Heaven has been invested in Him. Jesus did *nothing* without God the Father. He only ever did what He saw His Father in Heaven doing and only said what the Father was saying; He only went where the Father was sending Him. Jesus was always *abiding* in the Father. Abiding means to dwell, to live in. Because Jesus was constantly one with the Father He was always perfectly in sync with Him.

In the same way, we are called to *abide* in Christ. What does that mean for us? It means *thinking* the same as Jesus, *doing* only what He does, *saying* only what He says, *going* only where He goes and *desiring* only what He desires. When we dwell or "remain" in Jesus like this, by living in obedience to His Word, then we line up with God's will in our thoughts and our actions. Jesus said,

"If you abide in Me, and My words abide in you, you will ask what you desire, and it shall be done for you."

(John 15:7)

The person who abides in Christ continually will know a real power in their prayers. Allowing God's Word and His Spirit to work in us constantly means that we even have the right to pray and ask God about our desires, because they will be His desires!

Think about this for a few minutes. The highest level of prayer happens when we are abiding in Christ, allowing His desires to infiltrate and take over our desires. Then, whatever we desire and ask for will be done for us. When we abide in Christ, allowing His words to direct us, our desires conform to God's perfect will. When this happens we no longer have to wonder about whether something is God's will or not – because our will is in tune with His. God's will for us will be obvious because we will be living directly in the centre of His purposes for us.

Sometimes, however, we pray with our best understanding of God's will as revealed in Scripture but the answer does not come. Has God forgotten us? Has He changed His will? Of course not! Prayer is sometimes a test of our faith. The question is, are we willing to continue trusting in God when our prayers seem to go unanswered? Sometimes what we call "unanswered prayer" is in fact God's blessing in disguise. God wants to develop maturity of character in us and this does not come with an "open sesame" attitude to prayer. Prayer is not a mechanical tool opening the door to immediate satisfaction at all levels and in all matters. It is deep communion with God in which we surrender to His often mysterious workings in our hearts and in the world around us. For that reason, abiding in Christ is the only way for us to enjoy a life of abundant fruitfulness. God values our relationship with Him above all else. Abiding in Him opens the way for our prayers to be answered and for God's perfect will to be done in our lives.

Glorifying the Father

This kind of living brings glory to God, which is, in fact, the first and primary purpose of answered prayer – *to glorify God's name*. Jesus explained this to His disciples when He told them that He would answer prayers offered in His name so that the Father might be glorified in the Son.

On earth Jesus lived for the Father's glory. His single aim was to honour His Father in everything. All His words and actions brought glory to God. This has not changed, even though Jesus now dwells in God's presence and He has been glorified Himself by being exalted to a position next to the Father. Even in this place of power and authority, Jesus is still living for the Father's glory. Everything He does is with this aim in mind.

When Jesus meets our needs it brings glory to God. When our prayers are answered in the name of Jesus, the Father is glorified in the Son. That is why Jesus promises us:

"Whatever you ask in My name, that I will do, that the Father may be glorified in the Son."

(John 14:13)

God wants you to be happy

Although many people seem to find it hard to believe, God wants to and does answer our prayers because He wants us to be happy! This may sound slightly flippant or superficial to some, but it is true nevertheless. Just like a father who wants to bless his children, give them good gifts and see them enjoying their lives, God is committed to blessing us. He so wants us to be happy that He frequently delights in granting our prayers and bringing our dreams and aspirations into being.

Some Christian teaching, especially in the past, has left people with the impression that not only must we petition God endlessly to get our prayers answered, but also that He is essentially angry with us, due to our sin, and that we have to earn the right to receive His love and blessing. To be blunt, a history of unbiblical teaching has suggested to numerous believers that God is a killjoy who wants them to be miserable and whose only method of working in their lives is through suffering. This is absolutely untrue!

In complete opposition to this idea, Jesus said that God wants our joy to be full and complete. He wants us to experience His peace and the goodness of His expansive blessing. This does not mean that we live our lives in a bubble, protected from any kind of hardship or difficulty, but we can do so with an overcoming spirit, secure in the knowledge of God's love and commitment to our well-being. We may suffer from time to time, but we know that wholeness and not suffering is God's aim for our life.

"In the world you will have tribulation; but be of good cheer, I have overcome the world."
(John 16:33)

It is of great comfort to us that there is no trial we can face that is greater than the victory Jesus has already won. Because of that, we can experience *His victory* in the midst of our own hardship.

From now on, when you pray, pray believing that God wants you to have joy and has your well-being at heart.

Have confidence when you approach God, because He is not searching for reasons to say no to your requests. Rather, He is longing to bless you.

"Until now you have asked nothing in my name. Ask, and you will receive, that your joy may be full."
(John 16:24)

Summary:

◊ One of the greatest secrets of effective prayer is abiding in Christ. When we choose to live constantly in Christ, listening to His will, His words for us, then our prayers will be in alignment with the Father.

◊ The purpose of prayer is to bring glory to God. An amazing reciprocal blessing is set in motion as we learn what is on God's heart and then pray that He will accomplish those things. God delights in answering such prayers.

◊ God wants us to be happy! God is not out to get us or to make our lives miserable. Rather, He wants to make us whole and bless us.

3 *Pray with Attitude*

Approaching prayer with the right attitude is important if we want our prayers to be answered. Someone has said that in prayer it is always our *attitude* that determines our *altitude!* In other words, we will never rise higher than our understanding of God's willingness to bless us. Prayer which breaks into God's presence and grabs His attention is prayer *with an expectant attitude*. Those who come to God with little expectation of His blessing are defeated before they even start.

A person who doesn't believe that God loves them, wants to bless them and answer their prayers, does not know His will for them. All these things are revealed to us in His Word as God's heart towards us. Effective prayer, therefore, flows from a living relationship with God and an understanding that His desire is to bless us. Prayer is personal, not mechanical. It is relational, not functional. It is a two-way conversation between a needy child and their generous, loving, all-powerful Parent. Understanding this will radically change our perspective of prayer.

But with this thought in mind, we must remember that prayer is not some selfish exercise in wish fulfilment. God always wants to hear us and answer us with provision for our needs. He is also prepared to fulfil the desires of our heart. But we must not treat Him like a divine slot machine or a Father Christmas type of God to whom we come with our shopping list. Jesus never said, "Come to me and tell me all your *wants* ...", He instructed us to focus on God's will and the priorities of His kingdom. When we do that, God is committed to providing for our *needs*. Prayer has much more to do with asking our Father to provide us with everything we need to carry out His will than it is about getting what we want.

*"But seek first his kingdom and his righteousness, and **all these things** will be given to you as well."*
(Matthew 6:33, NIV)

Do you know who you are praying to?

Because effective prayer flows out of understanding God's character and His heart towards us, it is vital that we *really know Him*. This seems obvious, but we have to ask ourselves honestly: *how well* do we know God? So much false information about Him has been spread about over the years that even the most balanced, biblically-aware of believers may have picked up a few wrong ideas.

One of the devil's key strategies is to slander God's character and integrity and coerce us into questioning Him. The enemy's campaign of lying and deceit is one of the main reasons why so many people pray from a position of doubt rather than faith and expectancy.

The Apostle Paul wrote,

"The weapons of our warfare are not carnal but are mighty in God for pulling down strongholds,

casting down arguments, and every high thing that exalts itself against the knowledge of God, bringing every thought into captivity to the obedience of Christ."
(2 Corinthians 10:4-5)

Paul reveals to us here that it is the devil's misinformation campaign that seeks to confuse us and prevent us from simply *knowing* God. Because the devil has been a liar from the beginning of time, false attitudes, ungodly beliefs and lies are deeply rooted in men and women. These lies take two main forms:

Lie number one

The devil's most successful lie is that God does not really love us or have our best interests at heart. This was the basis of his argument when he launched his first attack against mankind, seeking to deceive Eve in the Garden of Eden.

"Has God indeed said, 'You shall not eat of every tree of the garden?'"
(Genesis 3:1)

"God knows that in the day you eat of it your eyes will be opened, and you will be like God, knowing good and evil."
(Genesis 3:5)

Here the devil slanders God. He tries to convince Eve (and has been trying to convince us ever since) that God is cold, loveless and remote. He would like us to believe that we are the last person on earth in whom God would ever be interested. He would like us to agree with his suggestion that God is harsh and restrictive, someone who just wants to prevent us from doing things and having fun. Unfortunately, our experience as fallen human beings often *appears* to bear this out. Because such ungodly ideas are ingrained in our thinking we often seem to gravitate towards those things which are forbidden by God and we feel restricted when He denies something to us. We forget that *God has given us many better things to enjoy!*

Eve's response to the serpent was, "We can eat of all the trees except the one in the middle. If we eat from that one, we'll die."

"No you won't!" the devil countered. "God doesn't want you to eat that fruit because He doesn't want you to become like Him. God won't let you have something good!"

This was a terrible lie and a dreadful slur on God's character when, in fact, God was protecting men and women from something that would devastate them. Eating the fruit meant that humanity experienced evil and lost its innocence. The act of eating the forbidden fruit opened the door to all the suffering and misery which has ever been known in the world.

We must never forget this truth: God is good! He gives *good gifts* to His children and He only withholds from us that which is harmful.

Lie number two

The devil's second lie is to contend that it is God who is the liar and that His Word is untrustworthy. In Genesis 3:4 the devil directly contradicts what God has said:

"You will surely not die ..."

This is even worse than the first lie! The devil doesn't just throw doubt on God's Word, he flatly denies it. Every thought and word which causes us to doubt or disbelieve God's Word comes from the devil. His greatest goal is to smear God's integrity and he tries to achieve this by attacking God's Word.

The devil said to Eve, in effect, "Don't believe God! He's lying to you. You won't die." It is a tragedy that men and women everywhere have believed this same lie ever since. People are indifferent to God today to the extent that they think they can safely ignore Him. But ultimately we cannot ignore God and we cannot ignore His Word. What God says does come to pass. What He promises is fulfilled. All our actions have consequences and we will reap either good things or bad things from them depending on how we live our lives.

"Do not be deceived, God is not mocked; for whatever a man sows, that he will also reap."
(Galatians 6:7)

This is also the reason why our life of faith is so important and why our praying should constitute much more than presenting selfish requests to God.

A lifestyle of prayer

Prayer was never intended as an afterthought to the Christian life or something we do only when we are in trouble or great need. Prayer is a lifestyle – an ongoing, real time, interactive conversation with our Father in Heaven that covers every aspect of our lives. Prayer is instrumental in producing right living which flows from right thinking. Our heart attitudes shape us as a person;

they affect what we think, how we act, the choices we make. Most importantly, they determine how we pray.

"Keep your heart with all diligence, for out of it spring the issues of life."
(Proverbs 4:23)

Many years ago, I was seeking God for something that was really important to me. At that time, I'd seen God touch others through me in ministry and yet I still didn't truly know God's love for me personally. Because of this, I wasn't sure whether God would answer my prayers. Suddenly, the Holy Spirit spoke to me in my mind and said, "You don't really believe that I love you, do you?" It was true, I was convinced that God loved other people and wanted to bless them, but I wasn't certain about His love for me, and this heart attitude was spoiling my praying.

Are you like this? Do you think that God is more keen to bless other people than He is to pour His goodness into your life? Do you find it easier to believe that God loves someone else, than to grasp the fact that He deeply loves you? Allow the Holy Spirit to touch your heart about this matter now. Let Him minister God's love to you – His personal, intimate love, *just for you*. This is God's desire.

"Now hope does not disappoint, because the love of God had been poured out in our hearts by the Holy Spirit who was given to us."
(Romans 5:5)

God really does love you

We may ask ourselves, "Does God really love me?" but a better question would be to ask, "Why would God *not* love me?" because the Bible teaches us that God is love. In other words, God doesn't just "love" – *He is love.* God is the personification of love – it is an inextricable part of His nature – and His love for us is everlasting and infinite.

God's love is not nebulous or abstract, it is real, tangible and focused upon us. God has fixed His love firmly upon us, His children, and nothing can ever change that. God never does anything in half measures, so we can be certain that He loves us fully and completely with every bit of His being. The ultimate expression of His love for us was sacrificing His own Son to die for our sins. In Christ He has given us everything we could possibly need.

> *"When we were still without strength, in due time Christ died for the ungodly ... God demonstrates His own love toward us, in that while we were still sinners, Christ died for us."*
>
> (Romans 5:6-8)

God is holy. He cannot tolerate sin and hates it completely. Because of our sin we were at odds with God and separated from Him. But at the cross, Christ dealt once and for all with the sin and condemnation that plagues our lives. When we put our life into His hands, we are set free.

> *"There is now therefore no condemnation to those who are in Christ Jesus."*
>
> (Romans 8:1)

This means that God has demolished the barrier between us and Him and nothing can re-erect it. Those who put their trust in Jesus are now the beneficiaries of God's love. His love is ours and nothing will ever separate us from Him again. Whatever our circumstances and failings, whatever our shortcomings and problems, God still loves us and we need never doubt it. God always has our best interests at heart. Whenever He thinks of us, His thoughts are full of love. Every time He touches us, it is a touch of love. All His words and actions to us are packed with love.

God is good, the devil is bad!

At the risk of sounding simplistic, this truth can lead us to only one conclusion – one which we must hold on to at all times – God is very good and the devil is very bad. This may not be much of a revelation for some readers! But, to what extent do we really believe it? Is this the absolute and fundamental conviction of your heart? And if you believe it, what difference does it make to your praying, to your life?

The truth that God is good towards us, all the time, must dwell in our hearts to the extent that it constantly governs our outlook and attitudes. God is always good. He wills good, not evil. He promises good, not evil. He does good, not evil. This is the attitude with which we can come to Him in prayer.

"Every good gift and every perfect gift is from above, and comes down from the Father of lights, with whom there is no variation or shadow of turning."
(James 1:17)

Whenever anything bad happens in the world, people immediately cry, "If there was a God, He wouldn't let this happen!" This is a tragic misdirection of our frustration because the Bible is clear about the fact that God is not responsible for evil. He didn't create it and He didn't bring it into the world. In fact, He sent Jesus to undo it. God hates evil and He wants to put an end to it.

"For this purpose the Son of God was manifested, that He might destroy the works of the devil."

(1 John 3:8)

The word "destroy" means "to untie" or "unloose". In other words, Jesus came to undo what the devil had done. He came from God to do good and to break the devil's grip on your life, to break it forever.

"God anointed Jesus of Nazareth with the Holy Spirit and with power, who went about doing good and healing all who were oppressed by the devil, for God was with Him."   (Acts 10:38)

Satan is the enemy and the destroyer. He is the author of evil. But God's will for us is good. He never brings bad things upon us – that is the devil's work. God wants to remove and undo the works of the enemy.

Don't doubt God's goodness

Never let doubt creep into your praying. The Bible warns us against having what it refers to as a "double-minded" attitude. The Apostle James, who has a blunt, direct style of teaching, tells us that we won't receive any answers to our prayers if we do:

"Let him ask in faith, with no doubting ... For let not that man suppose that he will receive anything from the Lord: he is a double-minded man."

(James 1:6-8)

Remember, God is 100% good, 100% of the time. He doesn't bring us evil, and He doesn't send us affliction or sickness. Instead, He gives us good gifts, promises us good things, and keeps every promise that He has made to us in His Word. He sent Jesus to satisfy His holiness and reveal His love, and because of that we have full and free access to His presence. We are in the position where God can bless us abundantly because He has smashed every barrier between us and Him and swept all the pieces away.

These are the kinds of heart attitudes which get God's attention. When we approach Him, full of these heartfelt convictions, we can pray with absolute confidence and God will surely answer us.

Summary:

◊ The attitude with which we approach God will determine our level of expectancy. We must believe the truth that God wants to answer us and bless us.

◊ One of the devil's most prevalent strategies is to get us to believe that God is distant from us and indifferent regarding our prayers. We counteract these lies by cultivating a lifestyle of prayer centred on abiding in Christ.

◊ God has expressed the incredible extent of His love for us by sacrificing His own Son in order to win us back to Him. Because of this we should never be in doubt about God's love, commitment and goodness towards us.

4 When It's Too Late – It's Not Too Late

Life has a habit of throwing unwanted situations and crises our way and when unwanted or unexpected things happen to us, it is very tempting to say, "Well, it's too late to pray now."

Maybe some tragedy has taken place in your life and you feel that God can do nothing now to help you – that, because it has happened, you might as well accept it?

Perhaps you have been hurt and wounded constantly by others and you've prayed for God to change the situation, but He doesn't seem to answer your prayers?

There may be some other situation in your life that has caused you to resign yourself to the fact that there is no point in praying.

By no means do I want to appear to trivialise whatever you have gone through or are currently facing, but here is a truth that we all need to grasp: *God's Word to us remains constant despite our circumstances.* The truth of the Bible still applies to us, whether in good times or bad. This is why it is true to say that, in the face of every trial and difficulty, we are still *more than conquerors in Christ.* Though tough times inevitably come, these need not and should not derail our faith. The finished

35

work of Christ on the cross in our life is still finished. Nothing can undo what has already been accomplished for us in Christ.

God never stops loving you

God's love for each one of us is totally consistent. God does not love us more when we are being "good" or love us less when we are wilfully committing sin. Neither can His love for us be measured by our circumstances or problems. Sometimes we seem to think that when things are going well for us, when we are being successful, that God is busy lavishing His love on us. But this is a very dangerous way to think, because it implies that the opposite is true: that when things are going badly for us and we are facing difficulties, God has somehow pulled back and withdrawn His love and favour.

This, of course, is never true! God loves us immeasurably, more than we can imagine, and He loves us the same amount, constantly. We imagine that God's love ebbs and flows according to the circumstances of the day or perhaps according to His mood, because that is how *we* love! But we cannot superimpose our human understanding of love onto His divine nature. He has always loved us completely and fully. He never withholds any part of His love from us.

Nothing honours God more than when we are willing to trust Him *despite* our deep concerns and difficult circumstances. It is impossible to find the reason *why* certain difficult things happen to us, so in the midst of them we have to make a conscious decision to trust God regardless; to understand and know that His love for us is not wavering. Once we grasp this truth and begin to live in it, we strike terror into the heart of the enemy. The devil fears Christians who are prepared to trust God no matter what happens to them.

Remember the story of Job? Satan came to God throwing around accusations about his servant and the crux of his argument was this: "Does Job fear God for nothing?" Job was a wealthy and blessed man. Satan was insinuating that Job only loved God for what He could get out of Him. As this story plays out, it illustrates for us a vitally important truth: that God has chosen *us* to display the riches of His grace across the heavenlies. God has chosen us ...

"... that the manifold wisdom of God might be made known by the church to the principalities and powers in the heavenly places."

(Ephesians 3:10)

This means in practice that, like Job, we must continue to trust and love God through all the difficulties and tragedies that come into our life. Having this attitude is the very thing that will actually position us in the best possible place to receive His blessing. Once Job had learned this lesson, he began to pray for his friends and God restored to him a double measure of all that he had lost.

"The Lord restored Job's losses when he prayed for his friends. Indeed, the Lord gave Job twice as much as he had before."

(Job 42:10)

If you have suffered or are suffering loss or difficulty in your life, choose to honour God through it all. Don't allow yourself to be swallowed up by self-pity. Don't get angry at God and stamp your feet like a child. Don't wonder why this has happened to you and not someone else. Honour God, trust Him, pray for others and rejoice that God has chosen you to reveal His grace to invisible powers. When you receive and accept this truth, your breakthrough will not be far away and God may even restore to you double what you have lost.

Know God's goodness

The Bible teaches us that God's mind is constantly filled with good thoughts about us and that He is continually thinking of good things for us, so we need never doubt His integrity or stop trusting in His Word.

> *"'For I know the thoughts that I think toward you,' says the Lord, 'thoughts of peace and not of evil, to give you a future and a hope.'"*
> (Jeremiah 29:11)

When we really grasp this incredible truth we will stop looking all around us to see what our circumstances suggest is true and we will look to God alone. When we understand that "God is good, all the time!" as the old saying goes, we will cease to use our circumstances as a measure of His mind. Instead we will trust implicitly in His integrity and His consistency in dealing with us.

Once we understand the heart and mind of God towards us, we have the confidence we need to seek Him – to truly seek *Him* and not His blessing.

> *"Then you will call upon Me and go and pray to Me, and I will listen to you. And you will seek Me and find Me, when you search for Me with all your heart."*
> (Jeremiah 29:12-13)

Every blessing we could ever need is found in Christ alone. If we earnestly seek Him we will find Him – and on finding Him we will find the answer to our problems.

Seeking God means embracing Him for who He is and acknowledging His goodness towards us. We approach God with the certain knowledge that even if we come to Him in sickness, sorrow or oppression, His good thoughts towards us have not changed.

> *"For the Lord God is a sun and shield; the Lord will give grace and glory; no good thing will He withhold from those who walk uprightly. O Lord of hosts, blessed is the man who trusts in You!"*
> (Psalm 84:11-12)

Spend some time meditating on the fact that God is saying to you, "I am going to bless you, I'm not going to hold back any good thing from you." Let this fact rest deep in your spirit. God is good. He is full of goodness, full of integrity and totally faithful. God always keeps His Word to us.

God works all things for good

In his letter to the Romans, the Apostle Paul made one of the most amazing statements in the Bible; a statement that should fill our hearts with hope and boost our confidence and trust in God. He says,

> *"We know that all things work together for good to those who love God, to those who are called according to His purpose."*
> (Romans 8:28)

I believe, however, that this is also one of the most misunderstood and abused verses in the Bible, because Christians have interpreted it to mean something different than Paul intended. At worst, believers have taken this to mean that regardless of what happens in their life, they are to sit back and assume a position of passive non-reaction. They interpret Paul's words to mean, "When bad things happen to you, don't try to do anything, just let things take their course and somehow God will turn things around for you in the end." This is completely wrong. It is as ridiculous as a parent standing by while a wild animal attacks their child and saying, "Oh well, God will work this circumstance for good one way or another!" Any responsible parent would rush to their child's defence. Paul doesn't mean this at all.

What this verse does mean, first of all, is that God's good plans for your life haven't changed when something goes wrong in your life. *"I am the Lord, I do not change,"* He confirms in Malachi 3:6. Secondly, Paul is telling us that we have been called according to God's unchanging purposes before the foundation of the world and nothing can alter this. It means that no problem, difficult circumstance, sorrow or even satanic attack can separate us from the love of God in Christ. No harm, financial difficulty, sickness or tragedy can detach us from God's purpose to bless our lives.

Some people teach that Romans 8:28 means that sickness must be accepted as the will of God and that God will make good come out of this evil. I agree that God can cause good to come out of even evil circumstances, but this does not mean that we should sit back and accept the evil as if it was *coming from God.* Instead we should stand firm against the onslaught of evil in our lives, no matter what form it takes. Our enemy is a liar, a thief and a destroyer who wants to bring chaos and ruin into our lives. God wants us to treat the devil like a wild animal attacking our children – to deal with him ruthlessly and chase him out of every area of our lives. We have been given the authority in Christ to do this and we know that nothing he can do will ever separate us from God's love, power and blessing.

God has a good answer

So we understand that we don't have to passively put up with everything that the enemy throws at us. We also need to understand that it is not in God's nature to passively sit back and let the enemy have his way with us. All throughout the Bible He can be clearly seen as the God who intervenes. His heart is always to …

… deliver us when we are in trouble

… to provide for us when we are in need

… to strengthen us when we are weak

… to befriend us when we feel isolated

… to bless us for no reason other than He loves us!

We need to remind ourselves constantly that we are more than conquerors in Christ. Today, reading this, you may not feel like much of a conqueror. Maybe you feel stressed and troubled, weighed down by certain circumstances in your life? We all have different issues we are coping with in our lives, but we need to remember this: we cannot lose because the devil has already lost. Even if we are grappling now with circumstances that we feel the enemy is inflicting on us, these are a desperate attempt by an already defeated enemy to cause some havoc before his ultimate sentence is passed. We may be caught up in a battle, but the war has already been won and we are on the Victor's side. There is nothing the devil can do to change this. So even if you feel you've been shattered by life's circumstances, know that you are still a conqueror. God really is working all things together for good in your life.

God is not the source of suffering

It is true to say that as a result of living at present in a fallen world, we do suffer certain adverse effects. Bad things happen and we don't have a good answer as to why they happen. Some people teach that God allows suffering in our lives in order to teach us a lesson. I agree that sometimes God will use sickness and suffering in our lives in order to speak to us and instruct us, but this does not mean that the sickness or suffering is being inflicted on us by God Himself. This would be utterly contradictory to His character. That is not the way in which God cares for His children. He is never the perpetrator of suffering!

The truth that "all things work together for good to those who love God" is a faith-building, prayer-strengthening truth, meant to bring life and hope to us, not death and despair. It is actually promising us that God has a good answer for our worst problem. Remember that nothing can happen in your life without God's permission and everything that does happen to you will be turned around by Him for your blessing.

Summary:

◊ When we are faced with difficult circumstances in life, we should never say, "It's too late to pray now." This is the moment when we should pour all our energy into praying, because God's Word remains true to us no matter how bad our circumstances seem. In the face of the most adverse conditions, we are still more than conquerors in Christ.

◊ God's love for us is totally consistent and constant. When things are going well in our lives this is not an indication that God is loving us and blessing us more than usual or that we have done something right. Equally, when things are hard, this does not signify that God is displeased with us and has withdrawn His love and blessing. Our circumstances are just not an indicator of God's love to us at all! He never stops loving us completely.

◊ Like Job in the Bible, nothing brings more honour to God than when we choose to keep trusting Him despite our difficult circumstances. In fact, this deliberate choice is what will best position us for blessing.

◊ Dwell on the simple but profound truth that God is constantly thinking good things about you and of good things for you (Jeremiah 29:11). Determine to stop looking at your circumstances and to focus on God alone.

◊ God will take every circumstance in your life and turn it around for your blessing if you cooperate with Him.

But this does not mean you should accept evil as if it has come from God. God is never the perpetrator of suffering. Do everything you can in prayer to evict the enemy from every area of your life and trust in God to turn things around for your blessing. Remember that God has "good answers" for your problems.

5 Take the Devil to Court

In the previous chapter we looked at how we can trust God in every circumstance in our lives, even when it seems as though our prayers have not been answered. There are two reasons why we can trust God like this. The first we have already looked at: because God is committed to working goodness in our lives. The second is this: *because God is sovereign over everything to do with our lives.*

What does this mean for us? First, it simply means that God is in control of *everything* – period. Second, it means that nothing can happen to us in our life without His permission, because He orders our circumstances. He only *allows* things to affect us which He can use for His ultimate glory and our ultimate good.

We've noted the fact that this does not mean we should take a passive approach to our faith. In fact, the opposite is true, we are to actively engage with and seek to push beyond the obstacles life presents us with, trusting God all the way. The Apostle Paul viewed this struggle of the life of faith much like a running race and he used this metaphor in his teaching. We don't know for certain that Paul wrote the letter to the Hebrews, but this same analogy crops up in chapter 12.

"Since we are surrounded by so great a cloud of witnesses, let us lay aside every weight, and the sin which so easily ensnares us, and let us run with endurance the race that is set before us."
(Hebrews 12:1)

The picture that the author sets before us is one of a sports arena with a vast crowd gathered in the grandstand watching the athletes compete on the track. We can draw several things from this verse:

1 *We are surrounded by a great number of witnesses.* These are Christians who have run their race of faith and have already finished their course. God does not want us to indulge in what I call "grandstand" living, sitting as a helpless spectator in the crowd while the circumstances of life buffet us around. He wants us to be on the track competing. The only ones who are allowed to be spectators are those who have finished their race!

2 *We have to lay aside everything that might hinder us from running.* The fact that the writer of Hebrews identifies both "weights" and "sins" as things that will hold us back suggests that a "weight" is different from a "sin". In other words, there may be things in our life which are not outright sins, but distractions which are holding us back. A weight could be a preoccupation with our career or with a particular relationship that is preventing us from fully serving God.

3 *We are called to run with endurance.* Someone has said that the Christian life is much more like a marathon than a sprint. We are to run with perseverance for the long haul, keeping our eyes fixed on Jesus, who is our ultimate goal.

We are reminded here that we are permanently surrounded by a huge "cloud of witnesses" – saints who have gone before us. Scripture documents the stories of many of these in order to encourage us and provide us with role models to follow. These people proved in their day how trustworthy God was and we can do the same today, but we must get out of the grandstand and onto the field. This is the day for us to run with endurance.

Live on the front line

In order to ensure that we live continually on the front line of God's purposes for our life we must adopt an *activist* attitude. This goes further than merely refusing to be passive and always reacting when the enemy attacks us. To be an activist for God's kingdom means that we take the battle to the enemy. We set out to push back the enemy's boundaries in our life, never conceding defeat on any issue. We never give in and we never give ground.

Inevitably there will be times when it seems as though the enemy has the upper hand – we don't see a change in our circumstances, the sickness hasn't gone, the suffering still hurts – and at these times we can be tempted to think that something has gone wrong. There are two common reactions to this:

◊ Some people get angry with God, thinking that He has let them down.

◊ Others assume they have done something wrong and that God is judging them for their sin.

Neither scenario is a helpful way to think. First, we know that God's love is constantly with us and that He only wants good for us. Second, we know that occasionally

He allows difficult circumstances in our lives in order
to accomplish His purposes in us, but He is never the
source of them. Third, God never judges our sin
by sending suffering or sickness our way – that is
completely contrary to His nature. The truth is, when
things go wrong a battle may have been lost, but the
war has still been won. God can still take the worst
defeat you have ever suffered and turn it around
to work goodness in your life. Great triumphs can
come out of terrible tragedies and God can turn our
stumbling-stones into stepping-stones that, instead
of derailing our faith, carry us forward deeper into
His purposes.

There is a safety net

We can be eternally grateful that there is a safety net
beneath us when we dare to step out and live by the
promises of God, like a trapeze artist in the Big Top
of faith. Often we slip and fall, but we are caught
by the nail-scarred hands of Jesus every time.
Deuteronomy 33:27 says,

> *"The eternal God is our refuge, and underneath are
> the everlasting arms. He will thrust out the enemy
> from before you."*

This is how we should view God's sovereign control over
our lives. We need to live audaciously and not timidly,
launching out, aiming high, going for the big things. We
must believe God for the total and complete reversal of
every negative circumstance in our lives. If this does not
come about immediately, it is not because the promises
of God have failed. It may be that we need to endure

and persevere for longer, knowing that God's mercy and grace is available for us to draw upon at all times. His faithfulness endures forever and this is our fallback position when the going is tough.

The example of Joseph

Life has a very complex pattern to it and there are many different levels and layers of God's dealings with us. God calls us to fight the fight of faith in certain hope of victory, but whilst we are doing that in one area of our life, we may feel that in another area we are fighting a losing battle. When, however, we begin to see things from God's perspective, we will agree with Joseph:

> *"As for you, you meant evil against me; but God meant it for good, in order to bring it about as it is this day; to save many people alive."*
> (Genesis 50:20)

Joseph went through incredible trials on his journey of faith and it took a long time before he was vindicated by God. When we read about all that happened to him it is amazing to witness his incredible attitude to it all. First he was treated cruelly by his brothers and sold into slavery. Next he was abused by Potiphar's wife, who falsely accused him of rape, and he was sent to prison. But God was with Joseph all the time and he eventually rose to prominence in Egypt. Finally he was able to see God's hand on his life and from his position of Prime Minister of Egypt he was able to save God's people from starvation, including his own brothers.

We can think also about Jesus' suffering on our behalf. His rejection and crucifixion was the most wicked act in human history, yet it was also a vital part of God's plan to save the world and destroy the devil.

"This Man, delivered over by the predetermined plan and foreknowledge of God, you nailed to a cross by the hands of godless men and put Him to death."

(Acts 2:23, NASB)

Both of these examples illustrate the truth that it doesn't matter who intends to harm us, whether the strongest demon on earth or our fiercest enemy, God will still accomplish His purposes in our life and His will for us can never be thwarted, regardless of what our situation looks like on the surface.

God's pattern

God works in our lives like a weaver, threading a complex pattern into the fabric of our lives. It can take a long time and a lot of painstaking work before His pattern becomes visible, but when it does emerge it is glorious. When we get to Heaven we will be able to see to full effect the finished pattern which God has wrought in us and we will understand the depths of the miracles He has accomplished. Until then our life can sometimes appear to us like the wrong side of a tapestry – a confusing pattern of colours and rough stitching that does not make a beautiful picture – but eventually God will reveal to us the full extent of His beautiful weaving in our life.

"For I consider that the sufferings of this present time are not worthy to be compared with the glory which shall be revealed in us."

(Romans 8:18)

Love God, take the devil to court

God promises to work all things together for good for those who love Him. This means that if we continue to honour Him, believe in Him and obey Him, we will see victory in the areas of our life that are troubling us. But God promises us even more than that. God tells us that if the devil has taken something from us, we can press for compensation!

It may seem amazing, but God is in the business of restoration. His desire is to restore to us all that we have lost as a result of the devil's action in our lives. When we come to our Heavenly Father and ask Him to work His restoring power in our lives, it is as though we take the devil to a court in which God finds him guilty and demands that we are compensated for our loss. God has an incredible ability to work out a settlement to benefit us and to damage the devil.

Some reading this may be thinking, "I can't see how God can restore what I've lost", perhaps because your loss seems so extreme. Maybe you have lost a loved one, suffered financial ruin, or been afflicted with serious illness? But the message of Scripture is clear: it is never too late for God to act in your life and to work His mercy and grace in order to produce goodness and blessing. The devil may be a devourer, but God is the Great Restorer.

Abundant restoration

Under the Law of Moses thieves were commanded to pay back double, four-fold and sometimes even five-fold what they had taken by way of compensation, and in Proverbs God decrees that a thief should pay back seven times that which was taken.

"Yet when he is found, he must restore sevenfold; he may have to give up all the substance of his house."
(Proverbs 6:31)

God is so committed to blessing us that He commands an abundant blessing in return for the losses in life we have suffered. We see this pattern in the life of His servants in Scripture. Joseph was sold into slavery, cheated, wrongly accused, imprisoned and forgotten, but not by God. As Joseph placed his life in God's hands and trusted in Him alone, God released him from these dire circumstances and blessed him beyond his wildest dreams. In the nation that held him captive, no one was more powerful than Joseph than the king himself! But more than that, Joseph was used strategically by God to ensure the salvation of Israel and to preserve the line of the coming Messiah who would eventually defeat and destroy Satan's power on the cross. What an incredible privilege!

How can we apply these principles to our own life? No matter what the circumstances surrounding us, we keep on loving God, we keep on trusting Him and we never give up hope. Our God is a righteous Judge. Though many situations in our lives seem terribly unjust, God will administer justice at the right time and will find in our favour. We will be compensated by receiving abundant blessing from Him in due course. Don't be afraid to call the enemy to task and to bring your case before your Father. If you have suffered a loss, past or present, press charges on the authority of Romans 8:28! You can start by praying this prayer:

"Father, you know that I have suffered at the hands of the enemy. This is what has happened in my life ... [tell God all about the situation]. The enemy intended this for evil in my life, but You are a good God and You give good gifts to Your children. Please work Your restoration in my situation. Work for Your glory, work for Your good, and work for the devil's destruction. Amen."

Summary:

◊ Rather than taking a passive approach to living out our faith, we need to actively engage and push beyond the obstacles that seek to hinder our progress. The writer of Hebrews likened this to a race and encourages us to *"lay aside every weight, and the sin which so easily ensnares us ..."* (Hebrews 12:1). More than this, we need to be activists who take the battle to the enemy and seek to take ground.

◊ When times of struggle come and we don't seem to be getting any victory, we must not be tempted to get angry and blame God or assume He is angry with us. Neither will be true. Take your defeat to God and ask Him to turn it around for His glory and your good. God can turn stumbling-stones into stepping-stones.

◊ God has promised to catch us whenever we fall (Deuteronomy 33:27) and this should give us the courage to live audaciously and take big risks for God.

◊ God works in our lives on many different levels, weaving His purposes into the fabric of our being, as the example of Joseph's life shows us. Even though it took a very long time before he was vindicated by God, Joseph's attitude to his trials is a great example to us (Genesis 50:20).

◊ God promises to restore in abundance all that we have lost as a result of the devil's attacks on our life. Although the devil is a destroyer and a devourer, God is the Great Restorer and He can heal, restore and bring amazing blessing into your life, no matter what you have lost.

6 Praying with Faith

In chapter 1 we discussed the fact that prayer is never found on its own in the Bible, it is always mixed with something else. Prayer on its own is never enough to receive answers from God, it has to be combined with ...

◊ Confidence that God hears us and is willing to answer us

◊ God's will

◊ A godly lifestyle and attitudes

◊ Jesus' name

Later in this book we will look at occasions when we need to combine prayer with fasting, giving and confessing the truth. In this chapter, however, we examine how we can learn to combine our prayers with faith.

It is pointless to pray without faith. Smith Wigglesworth, the great British apostle of faith, was right when he said, "One prayer with faith is worth more than ten thousand prayers without faith." The Apostle James very clearly makes this point and shows us how vital faith is in getting our prayers answered:

"Let him ask in faith, with no doubting, for he who doubts is like a wave of the sea driven and tossed by the wind. For let not that man suppose that he will receive anything from the Lord; he is a double minded man, unstable in all his ways."

(James 1:6-8)

In short, it's not worth praying if you doubt God before you open your mouth. Prayer without faith is no more than a meaningless religious ritual and we can't expect God to answer us if we approach Him in a doubt-filled or double-minded manner. Of course, because of God's abundant grace towards us, often He does answer our prayers even when we don't speak them out in faith. But we should not presume on His grace – God is under no obligation to answer a prayer offered to Him in unbelief. It is an eternal principle of the spiritual life that God has designed grace to operate *through faith*, not without it.

As soon as we understand this principle and begin to walk in faith, believing that God is both able and willing to answer us, the doors of His grace are opened wide to us. Then, when we pray, God's provision is made available to us and all we need to accomplish His will is placed in our hands. God's love becomes our love in a given situation; His wisdom becomes our wisdom; His power becomes our power; His healing becomes our healing.

Receive from God

Some people find it difficult to receive from God. The key to receiving is believing. We start by realising and acknowledging that we were saved by grace through faith. This shows us that there must be some faith in operation wherever God's grace is found and that His grace must be present where there is faith. Only faith can guarantee God's promises – there is no other way.

"Therefore it is of faith that it might be according to grace, so that the promise might be sure to all ... "
(Romans 4:16)

The Bible tells us that exercising faith is the only way in which we can please God and that He will reward us for it.

"Without faith it is impossible to please Him, for he who comes to God must believe that He is, and that He is a rewarder of those who diligently seek Him."
(Hebrews 11:6)

This verse also shows us that there are two minimum requirements for praying with faith. First we must believe that God exists, and second we must believe Him to be a God who rewards us.

1. God exists

It seems incredibly obvious that if you are going to pray you must believe that God exists! And yet, I have known many people in life who didn't believe in God at all and yet prayed when they found themselves in desperate circumstances. I have also known of some atheists who prayed to God and He answered them! But this is because God always wants to reveal Himself to people who do not know Him yet.

Praying with faith, however, means more than just believing with your mind that God exists. Praying with faith also involves believing that God exists with all His divine attributes and capabilities. It means believing that

God is everything that the Bible declares Him to be. As God, He is the Creator and Lord over all; He is the only God and there is no other god besides Him. God controls all things, is everywhere at once and works everything according to His eternal purposes. God is all-powerful, all-seeing and all-knowing. Nothing is impossible with Him.

Do you have this image of God in mind when you pray? When you pray with real faith in this God you will see a difference in the answers you receive.

2. God is a rewarder

The second requirement for praying with faith is the belief that God *rewards* people who seek Him *persistently*. If you don't believe that God wants to reward your faith, then you will not come to Him with any degree of confidence, expecting Him to bless you. So we must recognise God's *goodness* as well as His *greatness*. In other words, it's no good being sure that God *can* bless you, if you're not convinced that He *wants* to bless you when you you seek Him and persist in seeking Him.

We will look at the key of persistence later in this book, but for now, please notice that to persist in our praying, even when no answer seems to be forthcoming, is vital proof that we are praying with faith. Faith clings to God for His power to bless, His willingness to bless, and His wisdom to know how and when it's best for the blessing to come.

Pleasing God with faith

We have already read that:

"Without faith, it is impossible to please God"
(Hebrews 11:6)

Faith pleases God. It delights the heart of our Father when we believe Him despite the setbacks we often experience. It brings Him joy when we trust Him during difficult times or when His answers seem slow in coming.

Effective prayer is prayer *with faith*. This is the kind of prayer that the Bible urges us to offer. It is prayer as God intends it to be.

> *"The prayer of faith will save the sick, and the Lord will raise him up ... the effective, fervent prayer of a righteous man avails much."*
>
> (James 5:15-16)

The effective working of God

Prayer mixed with faith has access to unimaginable power – the very power or working of God. Charles Spurgeon, the great Baptist preacher in nineteenth century London said, "Prayer is the slender nerve that moves the muscles of omnipotence." What a fantastic thought! When we pray, we move God's muscles! He rolls up His sleeves and begins to act powerfully for our sake. He flexes His might on our behalf or on behalf of those for whom we are praying. The Greek word *energeia* describes this process. It means "effective working" or "operational power". Prayer releases the effective working of God. It is the operational power of God in action. That is the awesome nature of prayer with faith.

One of the most inspiring books I've ever read on prayer is called *The Kneeling Christian*. In it, the book's anonymous author describes the things that prayer has and can achieve.

"Prayer has divided seas, rolled up flowing rivers, made flinty rocks gush into fountains, quenched flames of fire, muzzled lions, disarmed vipers and poisons, marshalled the stars against the wicked, stopped the course of the moon, arrested the sun in its rapid race, burst open iron gates, released souls from eternity, conquered the strongest devils and commanded legions of angels down from heaven.

Prayer has bridled and changed the raging passions of man and routed and destroyed vast armies of proud, daring, blustering atheists. Prayer has brought one man from the bottom of the sea and carried another in a chariot of fire to heaven. What has prayer not done?"

We understand, of course, that it is God who has done these things *through prayers prayed in faith.* John Wesley often reminded his followers that, "God does nothing except in answer to prayer." When it comes to prayer, there is a simple saying that reminds us our relationship with God:

"Without God, you cannot, and without you, God will not."

This is the privilege of the prayer partnership we have with the Father. This is why Jesus instructs us to pray with faith. Our prayers release the power of God on the earth as a visible demonstration that His kingdom is among us.

"Therefore I say to you, whatever things you ask when you pray, believe that you receive them, and you will have them."

(Mark 11:24)

Summary:

◊ Prayer becomes powerful when combined with other elements such as the confidence that God hears us, the will of God, a godly lifestyle and Jesus' name. Vitally, we must also add *faith* to prayer.

◊ Unless we pray with faith then what we have is religious ritual and we should not expect God to answer us. When we pray with faith, believing that God is both able and willing to answer us, our prayer life will be transformed.

◊ The Bible states two conditions for us to pray with faith:

1) to believe that God exists – but more than that, to believe He is who the Bible says He is: a loving and all-powerful God who longs to bless us.

2) to believe God rewards those who seek Him persistently.

◊ Prayer with faith is highly effective and will get results (James 5). It is effective because it will release the power of God to work on the earth in people's lives. Spurgeon called it the "nerve that moves the muscles of omnipotence."

◊ Prayer is a privileged partnership with God. Remember the saying, "Without God, you cannot, and without you, God will not."

7 The Faith of God

Mark 11:22 contains one of the most profound statements that Jesus ever made. This verse provides us with a key to our whole relationship with God because it reveals how we can move in God's miraculous power and how we can receive answers to our prayers. In this verse Jesus calls us not just to be *pray-ers*, but *participators* in the process of answered prayer.

> *"Jesus answered and said to them, 'Have faith in God.'"*
>
> (Mark 11:22)

To understand the simplicity and yet incredible power of this verse we need to examine the context into which it was spoken. Earlier in Mark 11 we see that Jesus was hungry and noticing a fig tree nearby He went to pick some fruit from it. When He reached the tree, however, Jesus saw that the tree had leaves on it but no fruit, so He cursed it saying,

> *"Let no one eat fruit from you ever again."*
>
> (Mark 11:14)

Jesus wasn't simply cursing the fig tree because He couldn't get something to eat from it. This scene and Jesus' actions were a picture, an illustration of something much more important. The fig tree represented dead religion, especially the religion of Jesus' day.

Fig leaves without fruit

Ever since Adam and Eve tried to cover their sin and nakedness in the Garden of Eden with fig leaves, men and women have been trying to "cover" their sin by their own efforts. In His grace, God took away Adam and Eve's feeble fig leaves and replaced them with a sacrificial provision of His own. God sacrificed some perfect, unblemished animals He had only just made and clothed Adam and Eve in skins. This points prophetically to the fact that the blood of Jesus, the innocent Lamb of God, would be shed to deal with our sin and spiritual nakedness.

Religion invented by man is totally inadequate to save us or bring any real change in our life – it always has been and always will be. No lasting fruit is ever produced by religion. It is as useless as the fig leaves were in the Garden of Eden. This is why Jesus cursed the fig tree. It was a reminder to Him of Eden and symbolic of all that is fruitless, barren religion.

The Judaism of Jesus' day had been polluted by the commands and traditions of successive Jewish leaders and had become incapable of delivering God's blessing. This is why Israel failed to recognise the Messiah when He came.

But it is not only the Jews whose religion separates them from God when it should bring them closer to Him. Jesus is opposed to every religion which is founded on a "fig leaf" mentality – in other words, it has human effort at its centre and is based on human wisdom instead of the wisdom of God and the truth of His Word.

God wants us to reach beyond our ideas, our ambitions and our self-centred desires. In prayer He wants us to take hold of Him and the revelation of His Word. Faith is believing God. It is both personal and relational. It is a transaction between *you* and *God*. Prayer is you clinging to Him and this is why faith ultimately engages and then releases God's power. Religion substitutes human effort for God's power. It is fig leaves with no fruit.

God hates religious prayers

Human religion will always fail us faster than fig leaves on a frosty day. This is especially true when it comes to prayer. God hates religious prayers and He never answers them. Only heartfelt, sincere prayers arising from pure motives move Him to act on our behalf. God wants more than anything else to deliver us from any and every form of empty, religious tradition, so that our prayer relationship with Him will become more effective.

Though it may cause us to cringe somewhat, it is useful to take inventory of our prayer life at times and check to see whether we have picked up habits which are no more than "religious traditions". Think through the following questions and ask yourself honestly how many of these are true for you.

Do you think that God's answers to prayers depend on:

◊ *The way that you pray* – are you more likely to get answers if you kneel, close your eyes, hold your hands in a certain position, etc?

◊ *How long you pray* – do you think God would be more likely to answer your prayers if you spent longer praying?

◊ *When you pray* – should you always pray first thing in the morning, or last thing at night before going to sleep, or before setting off to drive somewhere?

◊ *How often you pray* – are answers more likely if you pray regularly than if you are more sporadic?

◊ *Your style of prayer* – is noisy, energetic prayer more effective than quiet, contemplative prayer?

◊ *The words that you use* – do you tend to use "special" words in prayer or phrases that you feel "get to" God more than others?

We humans have a terrible habit of trying to come up with formulas. We like to figure out how various things in life work and establish a process for them which we then slavishly follow. Although prayer is a dynamic, life-changing, interactive conversation with the living God, we are often guilty of trying to find and apply a "prayer formula" that works for us. If we have a simple formula, we think to ourselves, then we can use it over and over and get quick answers to our prayers.

If you have a tendency towards any of the prayer traits listed above, it suggests that you have fallen into a pattern of praying that is formulaic and your prayer life has lost some of its vibrancy. Real prayer is not any of the things listed above and none of these things are important to God. Prayer is all about the way in which God operates in our life to transform us as a person, and it is the vehicle through which He desires to bring His will into the earthly realm. Dynamic prayer is prayer that is energised, empowered and directed by the Holy Spirit. Human ideas and methods have nothing to do with it.

There is a simple difference between fruitless, religious prayers and godly prayers prayed with faith: real prayer flows from *genuine cooperation with God.* Religious prayer does not. Authentic prayer makes us God's prayer partners. This realisation should blow away all our religious ideas about prayer and how to get answers. Prayer is no longer about what I want, what I need, it is about engaging with the heart of God, praying in accord with His will and then seeing His mighty power released on the earth to change lives and situations.

The fig tree withers

The account in Mark's Gospel tells us that the day after Jesus had cursed the fig tree, the disciples were astonished to see that it had withered and died.

> *"And Peter, remembering, said to Him, 'Rabbi, look! The fig tree which You cursed has withered away.'"*
> (Mark 11:21)

The disciples, coming from a Jewish religious background, were on a steep learning curve to discern the difference between religion and real, dynamic faith, and it is almost as if Peter was saying here, "Lord, how did You do that?" We might have expected Jesus to respond to Peter by saying that he shouldn't be concerned with the dynamics of the miracle, that he should focus instead on its deep spiritual significance – but Jesus has a surprising answer. He says,

> *"You must have faith in God."*

Jesus is addressing all His disciples here, because the word "you" is plural. In other words, He is telling them, "You all have to learn to do what I've done." Jesus knew that His disciples would have to face "religious" opponents wherever they went and that they would have to be able to demonstrate the power and reality of God's kingdom – just as He had done – after He had finally returned to Heaven. This was their calling in God.

We have the same exact calling. We are called to demonstrate that the kingdom of God is real, here and now, and to do the works of Jesus on earth in our day. We are called to be "Good News" to everyone we come into contact with. We cannot do this without engaging and releasing the miracle-working power of God through prayer.

The majority of people today are fed up with what they perceive as irrelevant, boring religion that is disconnected from the real world and doesn't achieve anything. That is how many people view what they believe the Church has to offer. But nothing destroys empty religion and people's false perceptions of Jesus faster than a clear demonstration of the supernatural power of God.

God's power exposes the barrenness of human religion. Through your prayer relationship with God He may give you a word of knowledge about someone that gets their attention, or a release of faith to pray for healing for someone who doesn't yet believe in God. When the supernatural invades the natural realm through prayer, it has a dynamic effect. Lives are changed as the reality of God's power becomes apparent. Religious people hate such teaching on faith, because religion tries to put God in a box and make Him predictable. God is not predictable and His power cannot be contained! He longs to miraculously transform people's lives, but

He has committed Himself to doing that through you and me.

Have God's faith

If we look more closely at Jesus' words we find an even deeper revelation. Our English translations of Mark 11:22 read,

"Have faith in God."

The Greek language uses different letters to most European languages, but if we transliterate Jesus' words into English letters they read *Echete pistin Theou* which literally means: *"Have* [a command] *faith of God.* So the Greek New Testament literally reads,

"Have the faith of God."

or, better still,

"Have God's faith."

This is the kind of faith that Jesus commands us to have.

God's own faith at work in us

This sounds somewhat impossible at first and no doubt causes us to wonder, "How can I possibly have God's faith?" But this is what the verse means and it is completely consistent with its context. Jesus is teaching His disciples, and us, that they cannot just pray and expect to see things happen, they *must move in the miraculous power of God.* We cannot do the work of God without the faith of God, so we must cooperate with Him and always seek to move in *supernatural prayer*. This means following the example of Jesus, who continually sought to "copy" what He saw His Father doing. He learned to do this by spending long periods of time just seeking God's face and listening to what He had to say.

When God moves in His power through us, He offers us a tiny portion of His power which is equal to the need before us. For example, when He gives us a word of knowledge or wisdom, He gives us a fraction of His own insight in these areas. This is true for everything that God does through us. We cannot truly love others in a pure, Christlike way, without God's love working through us. We cannot prophesy without God's Word being in us. We cannot heal others unless God's healing power is poured out through us. It is the same with faith. Neither can we move in faith without God's faith at work in us.

God has confidence in His Word

What does it really mean to have "God's faith"? Faith has to do with God's Word. *It is simply believing Him and taking Him at His Word.* It means we have confidence that God is speaking the absolute truth when He reveals His Word to us, and that we are fully convinced that God will keep His Word to us.

Above anyone else, the one person who has total and unflinching confidence in God's Word is God Himself. When He speaks, He has complete confidence in His own integrity to speak the truth and in His ability to fulfil His own Word. Because God is God, He knows absolutely, without a shadow of doubt, that what He says will come to pass exactly as He declares it.

This total and utter confidence God has in Himself is what we are offered a fraction of. God gives us the gift of faith, which is a portion of the faith that He Himself has in His own Word. I can't emphasise enough how important this is for us to understand.

Use God's faith

When we learn to receive God's faith, we move out from the natural realm into the supernatural realm of divine power and ability. This is supernatural prayer. By receiving God's faith we enter into a partnership with Him that means we can pray the impossible and see it happen! The truth is, God's Word is as powerful through our mouth as it is through His mouth when it is spoken in faith under the anointing of the Holy Spirit. This is how Jesus withered the fig tree – He was cooperating with God. Being fully God as well as fully man, Jesus could have spoken out of His deity and achieved the same thing, but He chose not to work in this way while He was on the earth. Instead, as a man, Jesus did only what He saw His Father doing.

> *"Jesus answered and said to them, 'Most assuredly, I say to you, the Son can do nothing of Himself, but what He sees the Father do; for whatever He does, the Son also does in like manner.'"*
>
> (John 5:19)

Jesus was empowered by the Father through the anointing of the Holy Spirit which He received at the time of His baptism. He came as the perfect man, showing us how to live and minister before God. Jesus left us a wonderful example to follow. He said,

"If you can believe, all things are possible to him who believes."

(Mark 9:23)

On one occasion, when Jesus' disciples failed to cast out a demon and asked Him why they had been unsuccessful, He told them:

"Because of your unbelief; for assuredly, I say to you, if you have faith as a mustard seed, you will say to this mountain, 'Move from here to there,' and it will move; and nothing will be impossible for you."

(Matthew 17:20)

No one can achieve such miracles without knowing God, His Word and His power. We must, therefore, surrender ourselves to God's Spirit and allow God's faith to work in us through Him.

Summary:

◊ Jesus revealed to us the secret of moving in God's miraculous power, just as He did, when He cursed a fig tree and overnight it withered and died. It is simply and yet deeply profound. He commanded us to, *"Have faith in God."*

◊ This act was symbolic and through it Jesus was cursing all "dead religion" that masquerades as a true relationship with God. No lasting fruit is ever produced by religion because it is based on man's own efforts and not on the truth of God's Word. It is poor substitute for a living, active relationship with the Living God.

◊ Praying that is formulaic and "religious" is completely ineffective because God does not answer sterile, religious prayers. Real prayer happens when we reach beyond our selfish ideas and ambitions and cling to God, understanding His heart and having a desire to see His power released on the earth.

◊ Real prayer flows from a genuine desire to cooperate with God. Authentic prayer makes us God's "prayer partners" and prayer becomes about engaging with the heart of God to see lives and situations changed for His glory.

◊ When His disciples asked Jesus how He had been able to wither the fig tree, He answered, "You must have faith in God." This can be translated "You must have the faith of God" or "God's faith". Having God's faith means to cooperate with Him and to move in supernatural prayer, always seeking to "say what the Father is saying" and "do what the Father is doing" as Jesus did.

◊ To have "God's faith" also means to express absolute confidence in God and in His Word – to have, in some measure, the same level of confidence in God's Word as He does Himself. God's Word is as powerful through your mouth as it is through God's when spoken in faith under the anointing of the Holy Spirit.

8 *Praying with Vision*

God's people cannot function properly without spiritual vision. Throughout the Bible we read countless examples of God envisioning spiritual leaders who then instructed and directed His people according to His purposes. Through vision, vast numbers of believers were able to network together and achieve incredible things, pushing forward the boundaries of God's kingdom.

Proverbs 29 tells us,

> *"Where there is no vision, the people perish."*
> (Proverbs 29:18, KJV)

Vision comes when we receive a fresh revelation of God and it brings certain hope. Vision stimulates faith, releases power and inspires action. Without vision – in other words, spiritual sight – we cannot live the life of faith. This is why we need to apply *vision* when we pray. We have to learn to pray with our spiritual eyes wide open.

Hebrews 11:1 calls faith the evidence of things which are not yet seen. Faith operates by spiritual sight. Faith sees into the future and calls things that are yet to be, as if they already are. Everything that belongs to the spiritual realm is invisible to the natural eye. The realm of the Spirit cannot be grasped by any natural sense of seeing, touching or hearing.

> *"We do not look at the things which are seen, but at the things which are not seen. For the things which are seen are temporary, but the things which are not seen are eternal."*
>
> (2 Corinthians 4:18)

In this verse Paul explains why we need faith for our earthly life. Faith is our passport into the spiritual realm. In Heaven we will no longer have any need of faith, because then we will see everything to do with the spiritual realm *physically* as well as spiritually. But for now, we must trust God and live by faith.

We see Jesus spiritually, not physically

Jesus has not, as yet, been revealed to us physically, and yet by faith we already know Him. We are eagerly waiting for the return of Christ when we will see Him face to face, but by faith we are able to know and love Him now.

> *"... whom having not seen you love. Though now you do not see Him, yet believing, you rejoice with joy inexpressible and full of glory."*
>
> (1 Peter 1:8)

Because we have the evidence of faith we are able to rejoice in our knowledge of Jesus in advance of our revelation of Him at the last day. By faith, we already see Him seated as King on the throne of the universe.

The Bible promises a special blessing for those who believe Jesus without seeing Him physically:

"Jesus said to him, 'Thomas, because you have seen Me, you have believed. Blessed are those who have not seen and yet have believed."
(John 20:29)

"Seeing" faith

From the very beginning of His relationship with mankind God has spoken to people using dreams and visions. Once we understand the importance of spiritual sight, we can see why God consistently uses such methods to speak to His people. Spiritual "seeing" is essential to the faith process.

The patriarch Abraham embarked on a long walk of faith with God. After their initial encounter, Abraham found it hard to keep on believing God to fulfil His Word, since a long time had passed and God's promises to him had still not been fulfilled. In Genesis 15 Abraham, at that time still called Abram, puts his complaint to God:

"Abram said, 'Lord God, what will You give me, seeing I go childless? ... Look, You have given me no offspring; indeed one born in my house is my heir."
(Genesis 15:2-3)

In verse 5 we read how God encouraged Abraham and inspired faith in him to believe to see His promises fulfilled. This was achieved through a spiritual vision. God will do the same for us. When God gives us a promise, before it is fulfilled He will show us what it looks like. This "seeing" before we receive is an important part of the process of faith. Without this vision we will "perish" or lose hope, and our faith will not be living and dynamic.

"Then He brought Abram outside and said, 'Look now toward heaven, and count the stars if you are able to number them.' And He said to him, 'So shall your descendants be.'"

(Genesis 15:5)

God showed Abraham a vision of the fulfilment of the promise he had received. As Abraham looked up into the night sky, he saw a glimpse of the "finished product" and in this "seeing" real faith was generated. It was as though Abraham could see in those the stars the faces of all his descendants calling "Daddy!" In verse six we see the result:

"And he believed in the LORD, and He accounted it to him for righteousness."

(Genesis 15:6)

It was the same in Moses' day. God called the children of Israel out of Egypt to travel to the Promised Land. To begin with they could not see the land of Canaan with their natural eyes. They had to trust that God knew what He was doing and see it only with the eyes of faith.

Prior to their arrival in the Promised Land, Moses sent out spies to travel throughout it and bring back a detailed report. Interestingly, we read that most of the spies returned with a bad report, saying that the land was impregnable and that the people who lived there could not be defeated. Only two spies, Caleb and Joshua, had spiritual vision and viewed the land with the eyes of faith.

Forty years later, God took Moses up a mountain to show him the Promised Land. It was a spiritual vision of the whole land as well as a physical seeing of part of it. Why did God do this? It was partly just to bless Moses because God was showing him His favour, but it was also to inspire him as the leader of God's people, which would in turn inspire faith in the people who were about to possess the land. Moses was to encourage the people with a reminder of what the promise looked like. Joshua, Moses' successor, also needed a clear vision to increase his faith as he prepared to lead the people into Canaan.

Vision comes before possession

Spiritual vision always comes before physical possession. We cannot pursue something in faith until we can see it clearly! Yet, many people try to live their Christian lives without vision and as a result lack direction and miss God's purposes. If we are going to take hold of God in prayer, we must have a faith-inspiring vision. We have to see in our spirit what we are believing God for when we pray.

Prayer is a lot like an architect's approach to a building project. He sees the building in his mind before he begins to draw the plans. Eventually he will submit his plans and requests to a building contractor and work will begin, but it will be a long time before the building site begins to take shape. In due course, however, what the architect had in his mind from the beginning will come to pass. Now, what was once visible only in the architect's mind is visible to everyone. God deals with us in a similar way. First He gives us a vision of the finished reality and we "see" it in our mind. Then He calls us to begin "building" in faith. We build by praying in line with the vision God has given us and by implementing in the physical realm what we have seen in the spiritual realm.

Obey the vision

Spiritual vision inspires obedience. Throughout the ministry of the Apostle Paul he continued to be inspired and motivated by the vision he had on the Damascus road. This occurred when Jesus confronted Paul, called him into His service, and Paul obeyed the heavenly vision.

Are you obeying the vision of God for your life? Have you *seen* what God has in store for you and are you cooperating with His purposes? We constantly need to check that our praying is actually in line with the vision that God has given us and that we do not lose focus. Personally, I never feel that I can pray meaningfully for something unless I have first been inspired by a vision from God. Unless I am carrying the vision in my spirit, then I can't persist in prayer for long. First of all I need to *see* the answer. Faith constantly operates in picture form. The Holy Spirit will often inspire us with a visual image of some sort to accompany a word of faith. The eternal God, who exists outside of time, can already see the finished result that He is going to bring about. Once He gives us a revelation of what He is going to do, then we too can see what it looks like and we can pray effectively, asking the Father to bring about what He has purposed.

A vision of Christ

God has predestined you and me to be conformed to the image of Christ. Scripture spells out very clearly what we will be like and who we will be like when we are translated into Heaven. This means that here and now, we can get on with the job of praying, of shaping our lives by making good choices that are in line with that heavenly vision.

The same principle applies in all spiritual matters. We will never develop an effective prayer life until we learn to see God's answers before they come. We will never pray successfully for someone else's or our own healing until we have seen that healing accomplished in the Spirit. In the same way, we will never receive other answers to prayer until we are praying according to the vision of God.

When you set out to pray about a specific issue, first spend time waiting on God, talking to Him about it and listening to what He says. Make it your goal to wait on God until the Holy Spirit gives you a complete vision of the finished product – in other words, God's answer to your request in accordance with His will on the matter. Only then can you really begin to pray effectively. Once you realise that this is the way in which the Holy Spirit works, you will want to allow Him to *show you* the answers to your prayers before you receive them. Of course, you still have to pray, because God wants to build and deepen His relationship with you! But this will help you to begin to flow powerfully in faith and within a short while your prayer life will come alive. You will be excited about praying and you will enjoy watching God's answers match the vision that He gave you at the beginning.

Summary:

◊ God's Word teaches us that we cannot function effectively without a spiritual vision. This is true of God's people corporately, as evidenced throughout Scripture. But it is true for us as individuals as well. Vision is stirred when we receive fresh revelation from God and it stimulates our faith, releases power and inspires action.

◊ Faith is described in the book of Hebrews as the "evidence of things which are not yet seen". A spiritual vision, then, creates faith that God will bring something to pass that does not exist yet. It is "seeing" faith.

◊ God has consistently spoken to His servants using visual imagery, through dreams or visions. Seeing before we receive is an important part of the process of growing our faith. Unless we can "see ahead" we easily lose hope and become discouraged. When we develop spiritual vision our faith becomes living and dynamic.

◊ Vision always precedes possession. Unless we first clearly "see" something in faith then we cannot pursue it in prayer.

◊ Spiritual vision inspires obedience. Have you seen what God has purposed for you in your life? Are you praying in line with that God-given vision?

◊ Our prayer lives will be transformed when we learn to wait on God and ask the Holy Spirit to give us a complete vision of God's answer on a specific issue. Once we see God's will and the answer He desires to give us, we can pray effectively according to His purposes and we will begin to flow powerfully in faith as we partner with God in prayer.

9 Speak to your Mountain

We may have confidence in the power of prayer as an effective tool. We may have confidence in faith. We may also believe sincerely that God can and will work through prayers spoken out in faith. But, ultimately, we have to remember that we can only truly have faith *in God Himself.*

This is the essence of faith. It is about believing God and trusting only in Him. It is not about prayer techniques, methods or formulas. God's faith only begins to work in us when we turn away from self-effort and focus instead on the person and power of God.

We have looked at how God's faith works. He has absolute confidence in His own ability and integrity to keep His Word. This means that whenever He speaks, what He speaks will be accomplished. It is a done deal. God has such supreme confidence in the power of His Word that He can speak about things which do not yet exist as if they already do.

God's faith at work

Like an architect, God plans His work and then works out His plan. He first purposes an event or a course of action within the Godhead. Then He speaks it out and finally it comes in being. When Jesus told His disciples to have "the faith of God", He was teaching them this same pattern of operation. This was how He cursed the fig tree. Using God's faith He spoke authoritatively to the tree. We are called to the same operation of faith because this is how God accomplishes His will on the earth.

God continually *decides* then *declares*; He *establishes* and then *accomplishes*; He *purposes* a matter and then *pronounces* it into being. Jesus has called us to operate with God's faith in the same way, as a prayer-partner or co-worker with Him. This is our whole purpose and destiny – to move in the authority of God as His earthly representatives, hearing the will of God and making pronouncements on His behalf, speaking out and declaring what He wills.

Our words have authority and power

At the foundation of the world, men and women were given specific dominion and authority in the creation order. We lost that dominion when Adam and Eve sinned. Now, in Christ, this authority has been restored to us and we are called to declare the government of God.

When backed by spiritual authority, our words have incredible power. The writer of Proverbs noted that,

"Death and life are in the power of the tongue."
(Proverbs 18:21)

Since God has made us in His own image, this means that our words have power, just as His words have power. We influence events and the people around us by our words. They have the power to build up or to destroy. Imagine then the power and potential for influence of words spoken by a Spirit-filled believer, speaking on behalf of Almighty God. It is staggering.

When Jesus ministered to people, He rarely prayed over them in the way in which we "traditionally" pray for others. Instead He pronounced God's Word over their lives and whatever He spoke came to pass. With a word Jesus healed the sick, cast out demons, stilled storms, fed the hungry and even raised the dead. He had seen ahead of time what God purposed to do, then He spoke out God's will and it came into being. This is the power of the "second Adam" in operation and we have the potential to move in the power of God in the same way. Jesus spoke God's words with God's faith. He spoke out of the anointing of God on His life with the authority given to Him by the Father. We can do the same!

Adam's dominion

The first Adam was made in God's image to exercise dominion on behalf of God. Adam's intimate relationship with God meant that he was Spirit-filled, divinely empowered and wonderfully enabled to fulfil his high calling. It was God's plan for this dominion to be passed on to Adam's offspring, but he disobeyed God, the bond of intimacy was broken, and he lost everything.

Now Jesus, the second Adam, has restored dominion to His offspring – all those who have put their trust in Him, been born again by the Spirit of God, and who are joined to Him by faith. Now believers have been given the authority from Jesus to exercise the same level of dominion that He did when He walked the earth. When we appreciate the significance and depth of our calling, we begin to speak differently! We are called to execute God's will on the earth and to occupy the place of spiritual authority.

Prayer with ...

This truth serves to highlight a significant fact for our prayer life. We have already seen that we must combine prayer with other elements which "supercharge" it and make it effective. We have learnt that we can combine prayer with vision and faith. We must also combine prayer with an awareness of Christ's *authority* and *dominion* and, therefore, our authority and dominion as we work on His behalf.

Prayer working through our words

When we pray with faith, God gives us the capacity to speak into a situation the answer we are seeking. This is what Jesus meant when He said we could speak to the mountains in our lives. A mountain is any obstacle that stands between us and God's will for our life. Jesus commands us to deal with our obstacles, to speak to the mountain. God wants us to actively proclaim the answer to our prayers, once we have heard from Him, and then watch them come into being.

> *"For assuredly, I say to you, whoever says to this mountain, 'Be removed and be cast into the sea,' and does not doubt in his heart, but believes that those things he says will come to pass, he will have whatever he says."*
>
> (Mark 11:23)

The faith of God operates through powerful confession and authoritative commands. I am not advocating what many have called the "name it and claim it" approach to faith, because often absent from that theological approach is the concept of waiting on God and hearing His will before we speak. It is absolutely correct that we should *name* and then *claim* what is rightfully ours according to the promise of God, but only after we have received a heavenly vision from Him which encapsulates His will in a given situation. When the faith of God is working in us in this way, then we should obey Jesus' instruction and speak His answers into being. Remember that God's Word spoken through your mouth is as powerful as God's Word spoken through His mouth.

The faith of God in us means that we have the same confidence in God's Word as He does. All doubt is banished as the Word declared comes to pass.

"Therefore I say to you, whatever things you ask when you pray, believe that you receive them, and you will have them."

(Mark 11:24)

This command of faith is based on the conviction of faith. We believe that we receive when we pray and in that conviction we command the mountain to move, and it does move. Like everything in the realm of the Spirit and faith, this will often involve considerable persistence. Although He sometimes will, God does not always give us immediate answers to our prayers because He knows that spiritually we would grow very little if this were the case. Instead He requires us to develop our faith muscles through faithfulness and perseverance, so that He can mould, shape and refine our character and fashion us into the likeness of Jesus. So we must speak to the mountain and *keep on speaking* to it until it is removed.

If there are seemingly insurmountable obstacles in your life today, make a decision to attack them in prayer.

Begin by waiting on God and hearing from Him what He wants you to speak out on His behalf into that situation. Once the Holy Spirit has envisioned you with how and what to pray, begin to speak to that mountain. Don't just pray to God, but speak out loud to the mountain itself. Pray with faith according to God's will and *command the result* that you know God has decreed. If you keep on persevering in persistent faith, you will eventually have what you are declaring.

Summary:

◊ The essence of faith is believing God and trusting only in Him. It has nothing to do with techniques, methods or formulas. God's faith begins to work in us effectively when we relinquish all self-effort and focus on the person and power of God.

◊ God works by conceiving a plan and then speaking that plan into action. What He speaks out always comes into being as His Word never fails. Jesus teaches us the same pattern of operation: hearing God's will, followed by a speaking out of that will in the authority of the Spirit. Just as God purposes a matter and then pronounces it, we too are called to declare the will of God on earth.

◊ God created man and woman from the beginning to have authority and dominion on the earth on His behalf. That dominion was lost because of the fall of man into sin, but Jesus came to restore that dominion. Those in Christ can now operate under His authority and exercise dominion on the earth once again.

◊ When Jesus prayed for people He didn't just pray words, He spoke out *God's Word* into their situation and saw immediate and dramatic results. We have the potential to move in faith in the same way.

◊ When we pray, we should pray with an understanding of the authority that is ours in Christ. Praying with divine authority, because we are aware of God's will, supercharges our prayers.

◊ When we pray, God gives us the capacity to "speak into" situations the answer we are seeking, which is what Jesus meant we are to do when He told us to speak to the mountains in our life. Follow the process at the end of this chapter in order to speak to and remove the obstacles in your life that are hindering you from executing God's will.

10 *Praying with Confession*

IIIIIIIIIIIIIIIIIIIIIIIIIIIIIIIIIIIIIIIIIIIIIIIIIIIIIIIIIIIIIIIIIIIIIIIIIIIIIIIIIIIIIIIIIIIIIIIIIIIIIIIIIIIIIIIIIIIIII

We have already noted Proverbs 18:21 which tells us that, *"Death and life are in the power of the tongue"* and we have discussed the power that words can have when we speak them out. All of this serves to remind us that our words count before God. What we speak is vitally important because by those words we may either block our prayers or bring them to fulfilment. I am talking about *the power of confession.*

We need to learn to use the language of heaven when we speak, not just when we are praying, but at all times. Sometimes we will use very precise spiritual language when we pray, but then undo all that we have said moments later with a few ill-conceived, careless words. Often what we say *after* we have prayed speaks volumes about whether we are truly moving in the faith of God or merely spouting religious rhetoric.

> *"Out of the abundance of the heart the mouth speaks."*
>
> (Matthew 12:34)

If we pray sincerely and believe that a spiritual transaction has taken place when we have prayed, that belief should influence the way in which we continue to speak. This is our "confession" – our ongoing speech relating to the subject of our prayers. If we pray in faith and then cast doubt on what we have prayed in our conversation, can we expect God to answer such a prayer? No! We must maintain a *conversation of faith* after we have prayed and in this way we will see our prayers carried through to fulfilment.

Negative attitudes and pessimistic words undermine and hamper our prayers, serve to block faith and prevent us from receiving answers (see James 1:6). They shut down the flow of faith in our spirit, steal our confidence and strip us of the blessings that God wants to pour out on us. We must remember that, after we have prayed, God is seeking a spoken response from us that corresponds to the answer He has given us in prayer.

This principle applies to the whole of our Christian life. We believe in our heart and confess with our mouth. This is how saving faith operates – our heart conviction is accompanied by a spoken confession. This confession of Christ is absolutely essential for salvation, and the principle continues throughout our Christian life.

> *"If you confess with your mouth the Lord Jesus, and believe in your heart that God has raised Him from the dead, you will be saved. For with the heart one believes to righteousness, and with the mouth confession is made unto salvation."*
>
> (Romans 10:9-10)

Salvation is a process, not just a one-off event. We have been saved, for which we are very grateful to God, but we are also *being saved.* This means that we are called to receive new life by faith and then we are to live out this new life by faith. This is the reason why our spoken confession continues to be important throughout our walk with God, and here is another element we must combine with prayer: *confession.*

We get God's attention when we cease speaking words for their own sake and begin speaking the language of faith – the language of confession. By this, I don't mean we should speak flowery, *spiritual-sounding* words, but real words of genuine faith which come from deep within our heart as we express out loud our belief and confidence in God and His awesome abilities.

The confession principle

Whenever we have prayed through an issue before God, it is a good habit to develop to go away confessing the things we have asked for. We should speak about them as if they are already ours. This confession principle can be observed throughout the New Testament.

> *"He Himself has said, 'I will never leave you nor forsake you.' So we may boldly say: 'the Lord is my Helper, I will not fear. What can man do to me?'"*
> (Hebrews 13:5-6)

This is how we confess. First, we speak God's Word to Him in prayer, believing that it will come to pass exactly as it is written. Then we take that same Word and declare it boldly, publicly. Such public confession always accompanies a true expression of faith.

> *"Since we have the same Spirit of faith, according to what is written, 'I believed and therefore I spoke,' we also believe and therefore speak."*
> (2 Corinthians 4:13)

Believing and confessing belong together like a marriage partnership. They are two closely linked and fundamental ways in which we evidence and develop our faith. We learn to *receive* God's Word and then we *confess* it by the Spirit of faith. In the New Testament, the letters written by Paul and the other apostles were intended to be read aloud in the various churches to which they were sent. With that in mind, the writers often set out to encapsulate important truths which they knew would form a part of the confession of believers. Look at the amazing truths which Paul packs into Romans 8:29-30. He lists them for only one reason, so that we will open our mouths and make a confession of faith about who we are in Christ:

> *"For whom He foreknew, He also predestined to be conformed to the image of His Son, that He might be the first born among many brethren. Moreover, whom He predestined, these He also called; whom He called, these He also justified; and whom He justified, these He also glorified."*
>
> (Romans 8:29-30)

Look at the five great revelations contained in these verses:

1 **God knows you:** *"Those whom He foreknew ..."*. This speaks about God's deep and intimate knowledge of us – the advance knowledge He had about each one of us even before the creation of the world. Praise God that from the very beginning we were on His mind.

2 **God has chosen you:** *"He predestined you to be conformed to the image of His Son ..."*. Before the world began God had chosen us to become like Jesus.

This is our unshakeable destiny and because God has decreed it, it will come to pass.

3 **God has called you:** *"Moreover, whom He predestined, He also called ... ".* This is God's call to us through the Gospel of Christ. It is His invitation to us to take up every part of His purpose for our life and we have to choose to respond to it.

4 **God has declared you righteous:** *"Whom He called, these He also justified ... ".* We have been pronounced "not guilty" in the court of Heaven. Not because we have ever done anything to deserve being acquitted of our sin, but because God has declared us not guilty since Jesus bore the weight of our sins on the cross. Because of Christ's sacrifice, when we trust in Him we are declared righteous before God.

5 **God has perfected you:** *"Whom He justified, these He also glorified ... ".* We have been given a position in Heaven, reigning along with Christ. This is not yet visible, we are not yet completely perfected by God, but this verse describes our future position when we will sit with Jesus in His kingdom and reign with Him forever.

These five truths have been given to us in God's Word that we might declare and live in them. Overwhelmed by these staggering truths, Paul has to declare,

"What then shall we say to these things? If God is for us who can be against us?"

(Romans 8 :31)

And this must be our confession too.

Summary:

◊ The words we speak out before God are very important as Proverbs 18:21 reminds us. The words we speak can have the effect of literally blocking our prayers or helping bring them to fulfilment. This is the power of confession.

◊ We need to learn to use the language of Heaven whenever we speak, not just when we are praying, and learn that the words we speak in our everyday life are just as important as the words we speak in prayer. If we believe what we pray, this should be reflected in our speech *after we have prayed*. Negative or pessimistic words will undermine our prayer, but a positive confession that declares what God intends to do will release a greater flow of faith.

◊ The act of confession is instrumental in us receiving our salvation, and is a pattern that continues throughout our Christian life as we adopt the practice of speaking out words of genuine faith, expressing our trust and belief in God and His power to accomplish great things on our behalf.

◊ The "confession principle" is found throughout Scripture. The Apostles included vast amounts of "declarative" truth in their writings so that we would learn to speak out the truth about ourselves in Christ. Practice the discipline and *believing* then *confessing* and see how it empowers your walk with God.

11 The Apostle and the High Priest of your Confession

When you accepted Jesus by faith as your Lord and Saviour, from that moment on you were never alone again. No longer spiritual orphans, we have been accepted and adopted into the family of God and Christ has promised never to leave us or forsake us, no matter what. Jesus is constantly with us by His Holy Spirit, helping us and sustaining us in our relationship with the Father, and this is especially true when it comes to our prayer life.

One of Jesus' titles in Scripture is "Emmanuel", meaning "God with us", and He is constantly active in our lives as the "author and finisher of our faith" (Hebrews 12:2). He is the One who is faithful in everything and has always been full of faith for us. Whenever we have prayed throughout our entire Christian life, those prayers have been *upheld* and *sustained* by our heavenly High Priest, Jesus Himself.

"Therefore, holy brethren, partakers of the heavenly calling, consider the Apostle and High Priest of our confession, Christ Jesus."

(Hebrews 3:1)

97

The book of Hebrews presents Jesus as the Apostle and High Priest of our confession. Christ's two-fold office and function guarantees that our prayers will be answered as He represents our needs and requests to the Father. Jesus Himself takes on the role of the originator and sustainer of our faith. In His royal capacity as our heavenly High Priest He regulates and administers everything to do with our faith. He does so on our behalf in the presence of the Father.

Your Apostle and High Priest

As the great *Apostle* of the New Covenant, Jesus was sent into the world to establish the new order of God on earth. He ushered in the reign of God's kingdom in the hearts of men, establishing a New Covenant which fulfilled and surpassed the Old Covenant. Now, back home in Heaven, Jesus has become our *High Priest*, and continually intercedes for us.

> *"He ever lives to make intercession for them."*
> (Hebrews 7:25)

The Bible teaches us that Jesus is the *originator* and *activator* of our faith, as well as the *sustainer* and *perfector* of it. In other words, whatever He initiates, Jesus takes responsibility for establishing and maintaining. His God-given task on the earth was to come and reveal God to us. Now He lives continually in the presence of His Father and His task is to represent us before God, like a lawyer or an advocate.

> *"We have an advocate with the Father, Jesus Christ the righteous."*
> (1 John 2:1)

Jesus exercises His ministry as heavenly High Priest by constantly making intercession for us. He was given this privileged, priestly ministry because of His sacrificial death for us. Old Testament priests were, in themselves, powerless without the blood of innocent animal sacrifices. It was the shed blood of a flawless innocent which gave them the ability to come into God's presence, to exercise their priestly authority, and to act effectively on the behalf of those who needed forgiveness. Without the blood there could be no forgiveness and cleansing of sins.

"According to the law almost all things are purified with blood, and without the shedding of blood there is no remission."
(Hebrews 9:22)

Jesus pleads for you

Since Jesus went to the cross for us at Calvary it is no longer with the blood of bulls or goats that a priest pleads on our behalf in God's presence, it is the shed blood of the perfect Saviour, Jesus Himself. Jesus is qualified to plead on our behalf like no other.

"Not with the blood of goats and calves, but with His own blood He entered the Most Holy Place once for all, having obtained eternal redemption."
(Hebrews 9:12)

As our High Priest in Heaven, Jesus constantly presents His blood to the Father. It is His blood that pleads for us before God. Because of the shed blood of Jesus we now have access into the Father's presence. Through faith in Jesus and His atoning work on the cross, we are encouraged to approach God's throne of grace with confidence.

"Therefore, brethren, having boldness to enter the Holiest by the blood of Jesus."

(Hebrews 10:19)

This right of access means that we have a right to claim all the benefits of Jesus' blood. There is nothing that His blood has purchased which isn't ours.

Claim the promises

How then do we claim the promises that Jesus won for us by His blood? How can we enjoy all of those privileges? The answer is by faith acting through confession. We must speak out and declare the truth of all that Scripture says is true of us. This applies to every aspect of salvation.

"Being justified freely by His grace through the redemption that is in Christ Jesus, whom God set forth to be a propitiation by His blood, through faith, to demonstrate His righteousness, because in His forbearance God had passed over the sins that were previously committed."

(Romans 3:24-25)

God's grace comes to us through our redemption in Christ, which was purchased by His blood and is received by faith. This faith must operate through our confession.

"For with the heart one believes to righteousness, and with the mouth confession is made to salvation."

(Romans 10:10)

We have already stated that without confession there can be no salvation. Now we understand why Jesus is called "the Apostle and High Priest *of our confession*".

Jesus works in us through confession

The ministry of Jesus operates in our lives through confession. As we faithfully confess Christ, His ministry begins to work in our life.

> *"Whoever confesses Me before men, him the Son of Man also will confess before the angels of God. But He who denies Me before men will be denied before the angels of God."*
>
> (Luke 12:8-9)

This applies to every area of our confession. *Every* promise of God has been sealed by the blood of Jesus and He longs to release His power to fulfil His Word in our lives. But first, our High Priest is waiting to hear our confession. Not just the confession of our sins, which have already been cleansed, forgiven and removed by His blood, but our *confession of faith*. When He hears this He begins to release His power in us to fulfil His Word in our life.

Jesus confesses us before angels

Jesus said in Luke's Gospel that He would "confess us" before the angels of God. Why does Jesus say He will do this? As our Advocate, Jesus speaks on our behalf to the Father. But He also repeats our confession of faith to the angels for one very important reason: He is releasing angels to assist us and to work in the circumstances of our life.

By speaking out and confessing our faith, we activate Jesus' heavenly ministry to intercede on our behalf. He is so committed to "finishing" and "perfecting" our faith that He will dispatch a legion of angels to minister to us if necessary.

> *"Are they not all ministering spirits sent forth to minister for those who will inherit salvation?"*
> (Hebrews 1:14)

In the Old Testament, King Hezekiah made a good confession when Jerusalem was threatened by the Assyrian king, Sennacherib. Read Hezekiah's prayer very carefully and notice all the elements of his pure faith-confession:

> *"Then Hezekiah prayed before the Lord, and said: 'O Lord God of Israel, the One who dwells between the cherubim, You are God, You alone, of all kingdoms of the earth. You have made heaven and earth. Incline your ear, O Lord, and hear, open Your eyes, O Lord, and see; and hear the words of Sennacherib, which he has sent to reproach the living God. Truly, Lord, the kings of Assyria have laid waste the nations and their lands, and have cast their gods into the fire; for they were not gods, but the work of men's hands – wood and stone. Therefore they have destroyed them. Now therefore, O Lord our God, I pray, save us from his hand, that all the kingdoms of the earth may know that You are the Lord God, You alone."*
> (2 Kings 19:15-19)

What a powerful confession of faith! Hezekiah's words express a full and unwavering confidence in God

– that He is the only God and that He has the power to deliver. We must learn to combine our prayers with such confidence and biblically grounded declarations of truth.

Now look at the results of the king's prayer:

"And it came to pass on a certain night that the angel of the Lord went out, and killed in the camp of the Assyrians one hundred and eighty-five thousand; and when people arose early in the morning, there were the corpses – all dead."

(2 Kings 19:35)

This is the kind of awesome, angelic power which is available to us through the heavenly ministry of Jesus.

God's answer depends on our confession

Jesus cannot release His power into our circumstances, however, without our confession of faith. As High Priest, He only administers – brings to pass – what we confess. This is why it is so important that our words are faith-filled and not negative and filled with doubt. If we are always confessing our doubt, then Jesus is powerless to help us. He is longing for us to confess the truth of God's Word so that He may enact all the promises of God that are true for us.

How tragic that so few believers seem to grasp this. How often do people pray a prayer of faith, but then, a short while later, give up and express doubt because nothing seems to be happening? We must not fail to hold on to our confession or throw away our confidence in God. When we do, it prevents the flow of Jesus' high priestly power in our life and our prayers could remain unanswered. We must be aware always that confession is not some magic formula for answered prayer. No "technique" ever is, since God is primarily interested in relationship. Yet, we are called to persist in prayer and developing our confession will help. Yes, it is hard to keep on confessing what we believe and have prayed for when nothing seems to be happening, but we have to remember that faith is concerned with the invisible realm. Faith has nothing to do with our natural senses or feelings. Faith is calling into being that which does not yet exist.

We would not give up on prayer so easily if we could see what is happening in Heaven when we pray. The book of Revelation gives us an amazing insight into what is taking place, showing us that the prayers of God's people rise like incense before His throne.

"And the smoke of the incense, with the prayers of the saints, ascended before God from the angel's hand."
(Revelation 8:4)

Not one prayer we pray is wasted. As High Priest, Jesus takes care of them all. Right at this moment He is sitting in the Father's presence, representing us, speaking for us. He is there for us because He loves us and because we are precious to Him.

When you pray, pray with confidence in the knowledge that Jesus hears your prayers and carries them to the Father on your behalf. Like Hezekiah, don't just pray empty words, but make your prayers bold faith-confessions that declare eternal truths about God mixed with your requests. Let your High Priest hear your confession of faith so that He can release His power to bring about your answer, marshalling the power of His angelic forces to help you.

Summary:

◊ Jesus is constantly at work in our lives in a dual role: as Apostle and High Priest. His role as Apostle was to come to earth and reveal God to mankind. He is the Revealer and the One who activates our faith. As High Priest in Heaven, Jesus has now taken on the role of our Advocate and Intercessor before the Father.

◊ Under the Old Covenant, high priests had to approach God with the shed blood of innocent animals, but Jesus entered the Holiest Place by virtue of His own blood and it is His shed blood which gives us access to the presence of God. Now, because of the blood of Jesus, we can confidently approach the throne of grace.

◊ Jesus' ministry is to act on our confession of faith, releasing His power to bring to pass the promises of God in our life. He has at His disposal a vast array of angelic forces which can be directed to assist us as necessary.

◊ We can learn much from the prayer of king Hezekiah in 2 Kings 19. His prayer was energised with *faith-confession*. Instead of merely expressing his needs or crying out in desperation, the king brought his petition before God packaged inside a positive confession that expressed who God was and what He was capable of. Similarly, our prayers need to be laced with a powerful confession of unwavering confidence in the person and character of God.

◊ Our confession is vitally important because Jesus can act on what we declare in faith. If our confession is negative and filled with doubt, then we stem the flow of His priestly power in our life. But if we boldly declare the truth of Scripture and the promises of God for our life, the Lord Jesus can release the power of those promises in us.

◊ We can pray with the confidence that Jesus hears every prayer we pray and is waiting to carry them to the Father on our behalf.

12 Prayer as a Lifestyle

Throughout this book we have been learning that we need to combine prayer with other elements in order to make it truly effective. We have learned to have a faith-filled attitude when we pray and to include the language of *faith-confession* in our prayers.

I want now to remind you that prayer should be as natural (and frequent!) as breathing.

We should understand by now that prayer is not something that we do only when we are in need or when there is a crisis in our lives. Prayer is a continuous and ongoing conversation that we have with God. It is the lifeblood of our relationship with Him. Prayer must be an integral part of our lifestyle. The Apostle Paul encouraged us to pray without ceasing (1 Thessalonians 5:17). But although prayer is a lifestyle in itself, we know that it must be accompanied by a special kind of lifestyle for it to be effective.

James 5:16 tells us that it is the prayer of a "righteous" person that is powerful and effective. We need to realise then that we cannot expect to pray *effectively* if we are living *defectively*.

Our righteousness comes from God

We can pray regardless of the state of our soul, of course, but if we want our prayers to be answered and we want to flow powerfully and effectively with the Holy Spirit, then it matters how we live. We have to line up with God's character and standards. We cannot aspire to this by our own efforts, but true righteousness is *imputed* to us through faith in Christ. In other words, true righteousness is the free gift of God received by faith in Christ.

> *"... not having my own righteousness, which is from the law, but that which is through faith in Christ, the righteousness which is from God by faith."*
>
> (Philippians 3:9)

We have to learn to walk in the righteousness that Christ has given us. How can we do this? By constantly listening to and obeying the Holy Spirit's guidance in our life. We need to develop a sensitivity to the voice of God's Spirit as He speaks to us and gently corrects and guides us, empowering us to live differently. Paul tells us in Galatians 5:16,

> *"Walk in the Spirit, and you shall not fulfil the lust of the flesh."*

It also means coming frequently to God to confess our sins and receive fresh cleansing from Him.

> *"If we confess our sins He is faithful and just to forgive us our sins and to cleanse us from all unrighteousness."*
>
> (1 John 1:9)

This does not mean we have to strive to be sinlessly perfect before God before we ever pray to Him. If that were the case then none of us would ever be able to approach Him. But we should keep short accounts with God, ensuring that when we know we have deliberately sinned, we repent and seek His cleansing and forgiveness. We should aim to live right before Him and not wilfully disobey Him. We are not to harbour sin in our hearts or even the memory of past sins. If this is an issue for you, then pray and ask God to restore your soul and renew your mind.

Live like God

Being "like" God means to love what He loves and hate what He hates. It means that we connect with God so deeply that we begin to be moved by the things that move Him and we respond to people in the same way that He responds to them. Imagine what powerful lives we could live if we acted like God at all times.

God is love, so being like Him means living a life of love. But what does this mean in practice? As far as Bible is concerned, love means total *giving* and total *for-giving*. That is love in a nutshell. One of the most famous Bible texts of all tells us everything we need to know about love:

> *"For God so loved the world that He gave His only begotten Son, that whoever believes in Him should not perish but have everlasting life."*
>
> (John 3:16)

In this verse we clearly see both of the essential elements of true love. God's total, absolute, pure love for us is revealed in the *giving* of His Son so that we might be *forgiven.*

Love like God

Living right and being like God means living a life of *continuous giving and forgiving*. The Christian life is that simple and yet that challenging. If our prayers are to be effective then they must flow from a heart that is both loving and generous. Our prayers must originate from a spirit that is giving and forgiving. Then it will be true to say of us that,

> *"If God is for us, who can be against us?"*
>
> (Romans 8:31)

Never forget that God is *for people*. He is never negative, critical or judgmental. No one would approach a person whose character was like this to ask them for a favour! Thank God that instead He is loving, gracious and full of mercy. Because of this, we need to copy His example. We cannot expect God to listen to our prayers if we are harsh and judgmental in our attitude towards others, or if we harbour bitterness and anger in our spirit.

> *"He who did not spare His own Son, but delivered Him up for us all, how shall He not with Him also freely give us all things?"*
>
> (Romans 8:32)

God is the Great Giver, He is not the Reluctant Withholder! If He did not withhold His only Son from us, seeing that we were in desperate need of a Saviour, then how could He withhold any lesser thing?

Open your heart

God has already given us everything we need – that is the measure of His generosity. So we should not expect to receive answers to our prayers if we are being less generous and gracious to other people. A heart that withholds is a closed heart and we must have an open heart if we are to receive from God. When our heart is open to give to others and to forgive them when they offend or wrong us, then it is open for God to pour His blessing into.

If our heart is closed to others and we hold back from forgiving them or blessing them, then our heart is closed to God. We effectively block Him from accessing our heart and working in us. This is another reason for unanswered prayer. In the next chapter we will look at combining our prayers with *giving*, but here I want to explore the issue of withholding forgiveness.

Forgive like God

We have looked at Jesus' teaching about mountain moving faith in Mark 11. It is striking to see what He says next. After explaining that God's faith is sufficient to move mountains and bring great answers to prayer, Jesus teaches about *forgiveness.*

> *"Whenever you stand praying, if you have anything against anyone, forgive him, that your Father in heaven may also forgive you your trespass."*
> (Mark 11:25)

Then He adds this severe warning:

"But if you do not forgive, neither will your Father in heaven forgive your trespasses."
(Mark 11:26)

This has important implications for prayer. If we want to touch the heart of God in prayer and see the answers to our requests, then we cannot afford to ignore Jesus' teaching on this topic.

Forgive others or forget answers

Jesus says that God will turn a deaf ear to our prayers if we are harbouring unforgiveness against others. It doesn't matter how much we pray, what words we use or how loudly we invoke Jesus' name – if we are holding on to any bitter resentment or unforgiveness then our prayers will not move God an inch.

We cannot receive from God while we are denying the very principle on which we are depending – His forgiveness and mercy!

How do we receive anything from God? It is by grace, there is no other way. We don't receive answers because we deserve God's favour, we receive answers because God chooses to give them to us in His mercy and grace. Thankfully, God's grace is freely available through Christ, otherwise we would get what we really deserved and we would receive nothing except strict justice from God.

Be mercy-full

I always tremble whenever I hear people demanding justice from God. Usually they are demanding that God administers justice to those who have hurt them in any way, but asking for mercy for themselves! But if He gave them the "justice" they were asking for, they would not survive the encounter.

"If You, Lord, should mark iniquities, O Lord, who could stand?"   (Psalm 130:3)

The Psalmist knew that he could not force God's hand. He had no personal righteousness with which he could earn God's favour. He had to depend on God's mercy.

"But there is forgiveness with You, that You may be feared."   (Psalm 130:4)

Look at the result of God's mercy in the Psalmist's life: he *feared* the Lord – the kind of holy fear which keeps us from being bitter and judgmental in our attitudes towards others. None of us have any right to withhold mercy from another, because we all need so much of it ourselves.

This is the point of the parable that Jesus told about the unmerciful servant. Even though he himself had been forgiven a huge debt, the servant was unwilling to forgive the tiny debt owed to him by another servant. We too have been forgiven an incalculably massive amount, so how can we withhold forgiveness from someone who has hurt us? It is like being owed a few pennies compared to the debt of millions we owed which has been completely written off. Look at what eventually happened to the unforgiving servant in the parable:

"Then his master, after he had called him, said to him, 'You wicked servant! I forgave you all that debt because you begged me. Should you not also

*have had compassion on your fellow servant, just as
I had pity on you?' And his master was angry, and
delivered him to the torturers until he should pay all
that was due to him."*
(Matthew 18:32-34)

Then Jesus adds this solemn warning:

*"So My heavenly Father also will do to you if each
of you, from his heart, does not forgive his brother
his trespasses."*
(Matthew 18:35)

It is clear to see how seriously unforgiveness will hinder
and even completely block our prayers. We simply cannot
afford to hold on to any bitterness. If someone has treated
you badly, pray for them. Take the bold move of asking
God to bless them. If someone has hurt you, talk the issue
over with God and prepare to do good to them. If you hold
any grudges against someone or if someone has offended
you, forgive them quickly and move on. Remember that
unforgiveness does the most damage *to you*. It rarely hurts
the other person.

Don't hold on to bitterness

In certain Bible translations Psalm 66 speaks about people
"cherishing" sin in their hearts. It communicates the
image of someone holding on to an object and treasuring
it. At first this sounds strange. Why on earth would anyone want to treasure or cherish sin in their heart? Yet, I
have seen this in people's lives countless times and it is
particularly relevant to the sin of bitterness and unforgiveness. Often, when people are offended or violated in

some way, they will cling on to the offence and "guard" it in their heart. They would rather nurture the seed of bitterness that has been planted in their life than uproot it and deal with it. Psalm 66:18, however, tells us that,

"If I regard iniquity in my heart, the Lord will not hear." (Psalm 66:18)

We cling on to unforgiveness or bitterness because we prize our "right" to hit back. When we have been wronged we feed our feelings of injustice and hurt by cherishing the thought of getting even in due course. But this is sin and it must go. If we want to receive mercy from God, then we have to show mercy to others. If we want our prayers to be heard by God, and we long for Him to answer us in His mercy, then we simply *must learn to forgive.*

Be gentle with people

The teaching of the Bible is clear: we must never try to justify ourselves by exacting personal justice. First, we are in no position to become the prosecution, jury, judge and executioner for someone else's sins. Of paramount importance to us should be dealing with our own sins before God. Second, God is the only appointed Judge who can deal with the sins of the world. When someone wrongs us it does not go unnoticed, but God will deal with it in His way at the right time. Our best course of action when someone sins against us is *always* to commit the matter into God's tender hands. Paul spells the matter out for us very clearly in Romans 12:

"Repay no one evil for evil ... Beloved, do not avenge yourselves, but rather give place to wrath; for it is

*written, 'Vengeance is Mine, I will repay,' says the
Lord. Therefore if your enemy hungers, feed him; if
he thirsts, give him a drink; for in doing so you will
heap coals of fire on his head. Do not be overcome by
evil, but overcome evil with good."*

(Romans 12:17-21)

Simply put, two wrongs cannot make a situation right.
Human vengeance just makes matters worse. Paul writes
much the same thing in another letter:

"Let your gentleness be known to all men."

(Philippians 4:5)

His following statement deals with the issue of prayer and
shows that *gentleness* is another key to effective prayer:

*"Be anxious for nothing, but in everything by prayer
and supplication, with thanksgiving, let your requests
be made known to God."*

(Philippians 4:6)

The Greek word translated "gentleness" is a fascinating
one that really captures the essence of what it means to
be "gentle" to others in a Christlike way. It is a legal
term which means "a willingness to forgo legal rights
and suffer personal loss out of consideration for the
needs and condition of others."

Imagine the following scenario: a landlord takes one of
his tenants to court for unpaid rent and means to prosecute
her. In court, however, he learns that the woman's husband
has just died leaving her in financial difficulty, which is
why she is unable to pay. With this knowledge, the landlord
drops the charges against her and also writes off her debt.

This is the kind of "gentleness" that Paul is referring to – a generosity of spirit when dealing with others. This is an attitude which brings great joy to God's heart whenever we exhibit it, because it is *exactly how He behaves*.

Occasionally, when we have been wronged, and we move to forgive a person who has offended us, that person is unwilling to accept our forgiveness. There could be many reasons why they are unwilling, but it is vital that we release forgiveness to them, even if they appear to be unrepentant or unable to see how they have hurt us. Having offered our forgiveness, we must leave the matter between them and God. Our responsibility before God is to deal with any bitterness or resentment which is in us. We must not provide a resting place in our heart for unforgiveness. It will only stifle our prayers, choke our spiritual life and prevent God from giving us His answers.

If you are harbouring any bitterness or unforgiveness towards anyone, begin to pray right now and take it to Jesus. He has paid the price for your forgiveness, so with His help release His forgiveness to the one who has hurt you. This will bring a great release and freedom into your own spiritual life.

Summary:

◊ Prayer is not something we do when we are in trouble, though of course prayer is one of the best things we can do in any situation, but rather it should form an integral part of our lifestyle. 1 Thessalonians 5:17 encourages us to "pray without ceasing."

◊ If we want our prayers to be effective, then it matters how we live. In our lifestyle we are to emulate the character of God:

    – Live like God: we connect with God's heart and love what He loves and hate what He hates.

    – Love like God: we live a life of continuous *giving* and *forgiving*, and avoid being judgmental and critical of others.

    – Open our heart: a closed heart cannot receive from God, so we aim to live being generous and gracious towards others.

    – Forgive like God: Jesus warned us that unforgiveness will block our prayers, so we must learn to practice forgiveness towards others.

◊ All of us are in need of God's mercy in our lives, so we must practice showing mercy towards others. We have been forgiven an incalculable amount ourselves, therefore we are bound to forgive others as God forgave us.

◊ It can be very tempting to cling on to bitterness and resentment and to nurture them in our heart, but the Bible says that if we do this, God will simply not hear our prayers (Psalm 66:18). Instead we are taught to be "gentle" with people and to leave the issue of judgment for sin to God alone. Biblical gentleness is not just acting kindly towards people, it is a willingness to forgo our rights and suffer loss out of consideration for others. This is the kind of self-sacrificial living that God honours and He will bless you as a result of living this way.

◊ If you recognise that you have issues of bitterness or unforgiveness in your life, pray about them now and ask God to heal and release you as you go through the process of forgiving those who have hurt you.

13 *Praying with Giving*

We have seen that prayer which gets God's attention flows from a gentle, merciful lifestyle and that our prayers become effective when we flow together with Him, as Jesus expressed in John 15.

> *"If you abide in Me, and My words abide in you, you will ask what you desire, and it shall be done for you."*
>
> (John 15:7)

Through prayer God aims to develop the divine nature that has been planted within us, so that our character becomes more and more like His. Since God is love, He looks for signs of His love in us. As He is forgiving, He watches us to see fresh growth in forgiveness.

The giving God

As well as being forgiving, God is also a *giving* God. In fact, giving is the chief expression of His love. It is at the very heart of His nature. Consider the implications of this for prayer. If our heart is open to give, then it is also open to receive. If our heart is closed to others, then it is also closed to God and unable to receive from Him.

"Do not be deceived, God is not mocked; for whatever a man sows, that he will also reap."
(Galatians 6:7)

The principle of sowing and reaping can be seen plainly in the natural world. Farmers harvest from what they sow. When they sow corn, they reap corn, and when they sow wheat, they reap wheat. The size of the harvest is dependent on the amount of seed they sow. The same is true spiritually for us.

"He who sows sparingly will also reap sparingly and he who sows bountifully will also reap bountifully."
(2 Corinthians 9:6)

This is the basis for the Bible's teaching on giving and receiving. It applies to every area of Christian life and living, and it is particularly relevant to answered prayer.

Pray with giving

Throughout this book we have looked at various elements that combine with our praying to make it potent and effective. Now I want us to consider *giving* as one of those essential elements. This may be a new idea to many, but I believe that grasping this principle and applying it will revolutionise your prayer life.

What is true for forgiveness is also true for giving. We cannot come before God expecting Him to *give* to us, if we are not *giving* to others and are withholding blessing from people when it is in our power to fulfil their needs. The prophet Malachi dealt with the sin of withholding in his day – in this context speaking specifically about tithing to God.

"'Bring all the tithes into the storehouse, that there may be food in My house, and prove Me now in this,' says the Lord of hosts, 'If I will not open for you the windows of heaven and pour out for you such blessing that there will not be room enough to receive it.'"
(Malachi 3:10)

Malachi is an important prophet for us to read today because his ministry was active in the final days before the first coming of Christ. Like Malachi, we are also called to live in a season of preparation for the coming of the Lord. Never before has the need for prayer and the power of God been so urgent, with nations rebelling against Him. The people of God desperately need a revival of faith and power.

This means that we need to know, more than ever, the secrets of effective prayer. Like the prophets of old, we need to have *influence* with God.

The open or shut heaven

Yet it seems at times as though the heavens are closed. Although in many parts of the world God is moving in tremendous power, we are still desperately in need in the Western Church. If it appears that God is withholding His blessing and glory from the Church, there can be only one reason for it: *we are not ready for it!* We may think we are ready, but as far as God is concerned, we are not ready.

How can God open the heavens and pour His blessing upon us when our hearts are closed to other people and, therefore, to Him? How can God give to us when we are withholding blessing from others?

When God decrees an open heaven over us, prayer is amazingly easy. We see numerous breakthroughs and miraculous answers. Our prayers shoot up like arrows and the answers come thick and fast in return. If you want to see this kind of blessing in your personal life, as well as the life of the Church, then it is time to stop withholding and start giving to God and to needy people.

"Whoever shuts his ears to the cry of the poor will also cry himself and not be heard."
(Proverbs 21:13)

Look at the implications of this verse. It literally means *giving = answered prayer*. If we hold back from giving to others it will block us from receiving when we are in need. When we close our heart to others, the doors of Heaven slam shut above us. But when we open our heart to give sacrificially to anyone who is in need and cultivate a generous spirit, then God personally flings open the doors of Heaven and starts showering us with His blessing.

"The generous soul will be made rich, and he who waters will also be watered himself."
(Proverbs 11:24-25)

Although the topic of this book is prayer, I cannot stress enough how much the Bible emphasises the importance of money and giving, because clearly *giving* and *prayer* are inextricably linked. Withholding leads to poverty at every level of life, not just financially, but the truly generous person will reap prosperity from God, financially and spiritually. I am not saying that our giving *buys* God's blessing, but when we give sacrificially in honour of the Lord, we touch God's heart. He recognises that aspect of His divine nature in us and He is compelled to respond by blessing us.

Unfortunately, some have tried to corrupt this principle of giving and twist it to their own ends. Some ministers do suggest that our gifts – to God or to others – *earn us* blessings. This was the great sin of the Medieval Church, where church leaders sold "indulgences" when they wanted to raise money. They told people that their gifts had "bought" their forgiveness. This is nothing more than bribery and does not work with God. It is abhorrent to Him. Teaching like this is a sign of an apostate Church.

Then there is the sin of Simon the sorcerer – the man who thought he could buy the power of prayer for people to receive the Holy Spirit. Peter's response to his request shows how angry this makes God.

"Your money perish with you, because you thought that the gift of God could be purchased with money! You have neither part nor portion in this matter, for your heart is not right in the sight of God."
(Acts 8:20-21)

We can never bribe God and for that reason we must be absolutely clear: If we put more money in the church offering basket we will not receive more answers from God. We cannot buy blessing from Him. Rather it is our giving from pure motives that moves His heart.

Proverbs 18:16 teaches us that,

"A man's gift makes room for him, and brings him before great men." (Proverbs 18:16)

In other words, a lifestyle of giving and blessing towards others is likely to lead to prosperity. It may even lead to greatness, but we don't give out of a desire to be great or to get rich.

Jephthah's need for victory

Judges 11:29-40 provides us with a practical example of how *not* to combine our prayers with giving. Jephthah was a man who mixed his prayers for victory with a promise to give. But he vowed, rashly, to sacrifice to God the first living thing he came across when he returned from the battle of victory. Tragically, it was his daughter who met him first after the battle. Even so, Jephthah fulfilled his vow to God.

We must be careful that we don't make rash or presumptuous promises to God, but to add giving to our praying *only* in response to the genuine leading of the Holy Spirit.

Hannah's unanswered prayer

Hannah was a godly woman who desperately wanted a child. Although she had prayed persistently, she still hadn't received her answer from God. One day, however, she went to the House of God to pray and this time prayed differently.

> *"Oh Lord of hosts, if You will indeed look on the affliction of your maidservant and remember me, and not forget your maidservant, but will give your maidservant a male child, then I will give him to the Lord all the days of his life, and no razor shall come upon his head."*
>
> (1 Samuel 1:11)

Hannah had begun to understand that she could combine *giving* with prayer to get God's attention and move His heart to answer her need. Then the answer came quickly.

"Then they rose early in the morning and worshipped before the Lord, and returned and came to their house at Ramah. And Elkanah knew Hannah his wife, and the Lord remembered her. So it came to pass in the process of time that Hannah conceived and bore a son, and called his name Samuel, saying 'Because I have asked for him from the Lord.'"

(1 Samuel 1:19-20)

Hannah had learned a vital lesson of answered prayer. She mixed her praying with a promise to give and God answered her, giving her a son. After that she was able to have more children. Supernaturally something had been broken in the spiritual realm.

A widow's unmet need

At a time of drought and desperate need in Israel, a woman of prayer was asking God for a miracle of provision. In response to her prayer God commanded her to feed Elijah the prophet who himself was in need. God spoke to Elijah saying,

"Arise, go to Zerephath, which belongs to Sidon, and dwell there. See I have commanded a widow there to provide for you."

(1 Kings 17:9)

Elijah knew that the first principle for receiving miraculous provision from God is this: just do whatever He tells you without question! So he went and when he arrived he approached this lady. Knowing God was going to do something miraculous he first asked the widow to make him something to eat and then to make something for herself and her son, adding this prophetic statement:

> *"Thus says the Lord God of Israel, 'The bin of flour shall not be used up, nor shall the jar of oil run dry, until the day the Lord sends rain on the earth.'"*
>
> (1 Kings 17:14)

The widow's obedience to God and her willingness to add giving to her prayers meant that her prayers were answered by God in the most amazing way.

> *"She went away and did according to the word of Elijah; and she and he and her household ate for many days. The bin of flour was not used up, nor did the jar of oil run dry, according to the word of the Lord."*
>
> (1 Kings 17:15-16)

The widow's mite

In Mark 12 we read the story of the widow who put everything she had into the offering and impressed Jesus. He said that the two mites she gave (the smallest unit of currency in Jesus' time) were worth more to God than all the offerings of the rich. There were two reasons for this.

First, God is more interested in what we are holding back than what we are giving. According to God's standards, the rich people gave less than the widow because they held more back. Second, the woman's gift was valuable to God because it represented an audacious act of faith which arose from a desperate need. Once the widow had given her money, she had nothing left to live on. But she knew her God. She knew that *He was her provision*, and she gave depending on Him to attend to her needs.

The Bible celebrates this lady's faith and records that she "threw" the coins into the offering. She gave freely and easily, not reluctantly, because she trusted in the God who had already met her needs. Allow this woman's faith to stir your own and to encourage you as you seek to mix your own praying with giving.

Summary:

◊ As well as being forgiving, God is a *giving* Father. This is the primary expression of His love. He is constantly giving and we should seek to emulate Him in this. If our heart is closed to others, then we are not in a position to receive from Him.

◊ Giving is another of the essential elements that we need to combine with prayer. Proverbs 21:13 warns us that if we close our hearts to the needs of others, this will have the effect of blocking the answers to our own prayers when we are in need. In Proverbs 11:24 God promises us that the "generous soul will be made rich". In other words, we will reap a reward financially, but more importantly spiritually.

◊ Giving does not buy God's blessing, but our Father, seeing a reflection of His generous nature in us, feels compelled to bless us when we give selflessly to others.

◊ The example of Hannah shows us that when, from sincere motives, we add the promise of self-sacrificial giving to our prayers, God desires to bless and honour us. Often such a change of perspective for us will unstop some spiritual blockage in our life.

◊ The two stories about widows in Scripture teach us that God is committed to meeting our needs, so we need not fear giving. Both of the women in these stories gave recklessly, ignoring the seriousness of their own plight, but trusting that God in His mercy would provide for them. God did not let them down and neither will He let us down.

14 Build a Memorial

In the previous chapter we looked at the issue of mixing giving with our prayer. There is one further special aspect of giving that warrants a short additional chapter and that is *building a memorial offering*. Again, we must remember that this is not a formula or a method for getting answers from God. He is our Heavenly Father, not a slot machine!

There are two main examples of a memorial offering in the New Testament: a generous Roman Centurion and a woman with a jar of ointment. Both of these offerings established something permanent in the presence of God. This is what a memorial is: a permanent "remembrance" which acts as a kind of reminder to God, just as He "remembered" His covenant with Moses and so came to act on his behalf or remembered not to judge Israel through the memorial of the Passover. For us today, we need to understand that faithful, sacrificial giving, mixed with our prayers, can get God's attention so that He "remembers" us and acts to meet our need and answer our prayers.

Cornelius' memorial

The Roman soldier Cornelius was a devout man who feared God. He gave generously to the needy around him and he consistently prayed to God. The combination

of prayer and giving were already mixing together
in his life. We can see that such an approach to life is
appealing to God because the Bible tells us God sent an
angel to Cornelius bearing this message:

*"Your prayers and your alms have come up for a
memorial before God."*
                                               (Acts 10:4)

Cornelius' prayer and generous heart drew a dramatic
response from God. All the time he was giving he was
building himself a memorial in Heaven until the point
came when Cornelius had God's full attention and He
responded to his needs. When Peter met Cornelius he
reiterated what the angel had said,

*"Your prayer has been heard, and your alms are
remembered in the sight of God."*
                                              (Acts 10:31)

Look at the emphasis of Peter's words "... are
remembered". They are present tense – a present and
permanent reminder before God. It meant that God
would continually be reminded of Cornelius' needs and
then act on his behalf.

A woman with expensive ointment

In the Gospels we read of a woman who built herself a
memorial through her actions. She had in her possession a
very expensive jar of ointment. She may have received it
via a family inheritance or she may have been keeping it
as an investment to provide for her old age. But whatever
the reason, she was overcome with love for Jesus and her

chief desire was to serve Him, so she broke the jar and poured the fragrant ointment on Him in an astonishing act of worship.

It is interesting to note that she was immediately criticized for her actions. It is amazing how people will often pour scorn upon sacrificial acts of worship to God. Lavish displays of worship and generous tokens of love offend the worldly-minded, but they provide sweet and fragrant worship to Jesus.

Jesus defended the woman against her attackers.

"She has done what she could. She has come beforehand to anoint My body for burial. Assuredly, I say to you, wherever this gospel is preached throughout the whole world, what this woman did will also be spoken of as a memorial to her."

(Mark 14:8-9)

Jesus promised that this woman's sacrificial giving would be remembered, and it was. It was recorded in the Gospels for future generations to hear about. More importantly, this lady's offering was recorded and remembered in Heaven. She is now reaping her eternal reward.

You might wonder, how much would one have to give before God responded as dramatically as He did to these people? The woman's ointment was worth the equivalent of a whole year's salary, but that is not the point here. Jesus said of her, "She did what she could." An offering that you decide to make in order to honour God could cost you a year's salary, or it could cost one week's benefit payment. The amount is not the issue. Doing what we can to honour God and bless others is the issue.

When it comes to giving, listen carefully to the Holy Spirit and allow Him to speak to you about your requests. He will show you when and how, and how much to give and God will bless you as a result.

Summary:

◊ A *memorial offering* is giving that gets God's attention. As a result of "remembering" our sacrificial giving God will act to bless us.

◊ Cornelius' persistent giving could not go unnoticed by God, so He sent an angel to him with a message.

◊ The woman with the jar of ointment made such an extravagant sacrifice for Jesus that He promised her story would be remembered for generations and it has been.

◊ These examples should fill us with hope because when we give, our giving does not go unnoticed by God, and if we continue to give selflessly He may decide to specially honour or reward us.

15 Prayer and Fasting

None of us will ever fully understand prayer. It is a holy mystery and yet it is God's chosen method of working in our lives and on the earth. Because of this, we cannot impose our own ideas upon prayer and try to make *it* fit in with our understanding. We must follow God's Word carefully and apply its teaching on prayer to our lives.

Fasting is another element which we can combine with prayer at certain times and under certain conditions. Others have called fasting "the neglected discipline" and this is certainly true today.

Fasting is actually good for our health and more people should fast purely for physical reasons, particularly in the West where most of us consume far too much food. But this isn't the main reason why God commands prayer with fasting. We are urged to fast for the spiritual benefits it brings. Fasting is a powerful spiritual tool.

Biblical fasting has two main purposes. First, it is used to express a deep repentance for sin – a repentance that is accompanied by sorrow and mourning. Second, it shows God that we are serious about seeking Him. This is what links fasting to prayer.

Although it can be beneficial to fast, because it helps to flush toxins out of our body, fasting alone does not bring any spiritual benefit. It has to be combined with prayer.

Prayer and fasting put together form a powerful spiritual weapon. Throughout Scripture we see that the people of God fasted during times of crisis.

Fasting expressing sorrow

At times fasting can be our natural reaction to shocking news or trauma. It is common for people to lose their appetite and refuse to eat when they are in shock. But fasting can go much further than this as a way of expressing deep sorrow to God.

In Nehemiah's day, the walls of the city of Jerusalem were broken down and the city was derelict. The Bible tells us that Nehemiah sat down and wept because of this, because he felt the loss of God's heritage for His people so keenly. He mourned and fasted for several days. Clearly this was a time of prophetic mourning and similarly, we can mourn spiritually for ourselves or our church or our nation. Jesus said,

> *"Blessed are those who mourn, for they shall be comforted."*
>
> (Matthew 5:4)

Biblical fasting is often linked with mourning for sin and humbling ourselves before God. This is implied in this well known passage on repentance:

> *"If My people who are called by My name will humble themselves, and pray and seek My face, and turn from their wicked ways, then I will hear from heaven, and will forgive their sin and heal their land."*
>
> (2 Chronicles 7:14)

The phrase "humble themselves" here refers to fasting. The Bible never tells us to ask God to humble us, but instructs us to humble ourselves.

"Humble yourselves in the sight of the Lord, and He will lift you up."

(James 4:10)

When we do fully humble ourselves, God hears us and lifts us up. His desire is to pour His grace on the humble.

"God resists the proud, but gives grace to the humble."

(James 4:6)

Fasting is a good way of humbling ourselves before God, but we must not think of it as a "punishment" for our sins. It is not a self-imposed punishment, but rather a way of demonstrating to God that we are serious in wanting His rule established in our life.

Fasting shows sincerity

It is the physical discipline of going without food for a time that brings us health benefits. But the spiritual benefits do not lie in the act of denying ourselves food. Fasting is not a spiritual "hunger strike" to force God to act in a particular situation. The spiritual benefits of fasting arise from our determination to seek God single-mindedly. It says to God, "Father, right now seeking You is more important to me than anything else – more important than food for my body."

Fasting then, is almost a by-product of seeking God. No technique we can employ will ever elicit a response from God, but sincere seeking will.

Fast with godly motives

In Isaiah's time, the people of God had reduced fasting to a mere ritual. It had become a spiritual technique for them – a way of getting God to answer. They thought that their religious rituals kept God happy, but Isaiah announced God's shocking response to their attitude.

> *"You will not fast as you do this day, to make your voice heard on high. Is it a fast that I have chosen, a day for a man to afflict his soul? Is it to bow down his head like a bulrush, and to spread out sackcloth and ashes? Would you call this a fast, and an acceptable day to the Lord?"*
>
> (Isaiah 58:4-5)

Their fasting was not acceptable to God because it was carried out with wrong motives. Actually the people were pleasing themselves, not God. Jesus cautioned us about "religious" fasting too:

> *"When you fast, do not be like the hypocrites, with a sad countenance. For they disfigure their faces that they may appear to men to be fasting. Assuredly, I say to you, they have their reward."*
>
> (Matthew 6:16)

Fasting can be abused. We must ensure that if we fast, we do not allow it to become a religious ritual or a legalistic duty. The Bible condemns using fasting to impress others with the depth of our spirituality. This is exactly how the Christians in Colossae thought about fasting, but Paul corrected them, telling them that, in fact, the motives behind their fasting demonstrated their *lack* of true spirituality.

> *"These things indeed have an appearance of wisdom in self-imposed religion, false humility, and neglect of the body, but are of no value against the indulgence of the flesh."*
>
> (Colossians 2:23)

Whilst God condemns the improper use of fasting, He commends true fasting:

> *"Is this not the fast that I have chosen: to loose the bonds of wickedness, to undo the heavy burdens to let the oppressed go free, and that you break every yoke?"*
>
> (Isaiah 58:6)

The kind of fasting God desires is accompanied by a lifestyle of prayer and practical care for the needs of others.

Fasting achieves breakthroughs

In the Bible, people were usually prompted to fast when it was appropriate to do so. This means that we will be prompted by the Holy Spirit to know when we should fast. This prompting may come suddenly in response to an urgent need or it may come as a command to set aside particular times or seasons for fasting before God. If fasting is not prompted and led by the Holy Spirit, then aside from the physical benefits, we will probably be wasting our time!

Holy Spirit-inspired fasting, however, can lead to great spiritual breakthroughs. It can sharpen our ministry, release revelation and loose spiritual power. Through fasting God manifests His presence and releases His divine authority.

Jesus fasted while He fought Satan in the wilderness. The early Church fasted before making major decisions and during special times of ministry. Throughout the Bible fasting often preceded times of revelation which led to a great deliverance or victory. But it can never be used as a lever to make God act. David learned this hard lesson when he fasted unsuccessfully for the life of the child born from his adulterous relationship with Bathsheba. We must learn to fast with godly motives and to combine our fasting with godly care for the needy.

Summary:

◊ Fasting is another element we can combine with prayer to make it potent and effective. Fasting in the Bible is used to express a deep sorrow over sin that we have committed, and to show that we are serious about seeking God. In order to have any spiritual benefit, fasting must be mixed with prayer coming from godly motives.

◊ Fasting helps us to humble ourselves before God, but it is not a self-imposed punishment for our sins. Rather it demonstrates to God that we are serious about doing business with Him. Neither should fasting be looked upon as a kind of spiritual "hunger strike". We cannot twist God's arm to extract answers to prayer from Him.

◊ Fasting can easily become a religious ritual that ceases to have any spiritual power. God hates this, but He advocates the kind of fasting that results in a lifestyle of prayer accompanied by the practical care of others.

◊ Fasting can help to bring about spiritual breakthroughs, but we should only fast at the prompting of the Holy Spirit and be subject to His guidance.

16 *Praying with Actions*

We have learned that prayer should form an integral part of our lifestyle as we walk with God, but like with most other things in life we have to achieve a balance. The Apostle James warned about Christians who say all the right things but never actually do *anything* for God. The opposite is also true. We can be so busy doing things that we never take the time to pray, or we can be so busy praying that we never actually do what God is telling us to do!

Often, the key to receiving the answers we need in prayer lies in our hands. First, we must discipline ourselves to pray persistently about the issues we are bringing before God. But second, we must not neglect to do those things God wants us to do which will be instrumental in bringing our answers. It doesn't matter how hard we pray – we won't receive answers until we do what God tells us to do!

Do God's deeds

In the Lord's Prayer, Jesus teaches us to pray,

"Give us this day our daily bread."

(Matthew 6:11)

Does this mean that we should pray and then sit back and wait for God to drop a loaf of bread in our lap? No. After praying we need to go out and do an honest day's work. Our answer will arrive with our salary cheque at the end of the month!

Once, a young man came to me and asked me to pray for him to get a job. When I'd finished praying I told him that God had just given him a job. God's job for him was to get up early the next morning to start looking for work and to persist until he found some. The same principle applies in many other areas of prayer. It is amazing how many people expect God to answer their prayers for the salvation of their family and friends, and yet they never share the Gospel with them. Many people pray for deliverance from a particular bondage or sin, but they never introduce into their lives the disciplines and safeguards that would allow them to walk free from that bondage.

Pray with action

When we have prayed about something, God expects us to get up and begin doing the things which will help bring those prayers to fulfilment. Action may never be a substitute for prayer, but equally prayer must be accompanied by action. A. J. Gordon, one of America's greatest nineteenth century Bible teachers said, "There may be many things that you can do *after* you have prayed, but there is nothing you can do *until* you have prayed." This is the correct balance: first we pray God's will, then we do God's will.

Listen for God's instructions

When we are praying God will often speak to us and give us the keys to unlock our answer. Prayer is two-way communication. Prayer is as much about listening to God as it is about speaking to Him. When we pray, we should not just ask God to act, we should listen to Him so that we can hear what He is instructing us to do. Our praying should always include the request: "Lord, what do You want me to do?"

Never underestimate the wisdom that the Holy Spirit can give you during prayer. He will often show us how to pray and then what to do after we have prayed. God's instruction will come as the Holy Spirit drops a thought or idea into our mind. His revelation may come as a picture in our mind's eye or we may have a sudden inner feeling rather like a spiritual "hunch". God speaks to us in both these ways.

If we desire answers to our prayers then we have to learn to develop *listening prayer*. Pray with an open heart and an open Bible to check what you hear. Every instruction of the Holy Spirit will be perfectly in line with Scripture. The Word of God is living and active and God uses it all the time to speak to His people.

Obey your instructions

Prayer involves obedient actions – actions that fall in line with our prayers and which bring God's solutions into being. We must do what God instructs us to do, remembering that we cannot achieve anything without God's enabling. Remember the saying: without God, you cannot, and without you, He will not.

From time to time God will intervene and act on our behalf, as He did for the people of Israel when they needed to cross the Red Sea.

"Stand still, and see the salvation of the Lord, which He will accomplish for you today ... The Lord will fight for you."
(Exodus 14:13-14)

But even on this occasion God still acted through Moses. Yet, what God caused to happen was impossible without His supernatural enabling as the Red Sea parted and Israel crossed the river on dry ground. Moses' part in this transaction was to listen to God and to do what he was told. By acting in obedience, Moses experienced the enabling power of God.

The people also had to act; they had to go forward, but they went forward in God's enabling. The miracle needed the cooperation of God and His people working together. God will sometimes work *for us*, on our behalf, and He will work *through us*, but most commonly He will enable *us* to work the answer in our own life.

"He who looks into the perfect law of liberty and continues in it, and is not a forgetful hearer but a doer of the work, this one will be blessed in what he does."
(James 1:25)

This is the glory of prayer. As we pray, we develop an ever-deepening relationship with the Holy Spirit. God hears our prayers and releases His Spirit to enable us to accomplish the answer. If we learn to be sensitive to the voice of the Spirit and obey His instruction we will be given the wisdom to know what to do and the power to do it.

Summary:

◊ In life we need to achieve a balance between prayer and action. There is no point in praying without following it up with action, or acting without prayer.

◊ When we have prayed about something we then have a responsibility to act and to do the things that will help make our prayers a reality as the Holy Spirit directs us.

◊ Prayer is two-way communication. It is important that we listen for God speaking to us when we pray as well as us speaking to Him. Often during prayer God will impart specific insights to us that will unlock certain situations in our lives.

◊ Prayer involves obedient action. Having listened to God's instruction, we must do what He tells us to do. God will sometimes work on our behalf without us doing anything, but most often we will need to do certain things which are instrumental in bringing the answers we seek.

17 Don't Give Up

Maybe by now you are thinking, this is all too much for me to remember! Don't worry – prayer is actually very simple! It needn't be complicated – it is just asking God. Instead of wondering whether you are correctly applying all the elements we have looked at in this book, just allow the Holy Spirit to guide you and He will let you know when you need to combine one or more of these elements with your praying. But if you remember one thing, let it be this: never give up praying!

Persistent faith

Jesus told us to,

> *"Ask and it will be given to you; seek, and you will find; knock, and it will be opened to you. For everyone who asks, receives, and he who seeks finds, and to him who knocks it will be opened."*
> (Luke 11:9-10)

The tense of the original Greek means that these words are better translated, "keep on asking, keep on seeking and keep on knocking". It means that Jesus wants us to persist in our asking.

Sometimes when we pray, we just ask once and we receive our answer by faith. We just *know* that God has delivered our answer, even if we can't see it yet. From then on we just keep thanking God and speaking to the mountain of our circumstances to be removed. Any more asking is unnecessary because we have the Holy Spirit's witness that our prayer has been answered.

The prayer of persistence

On other occasions, however, we are called to pray and keep praying with persistence. This does not contradict the prayer of faith I have just described, it is just a different way of praying.

Jesus taught His disciples to pray and not give up. He told them a story about a widow and a judge to show them what He meant. In the story the woman was totally persistent in her attempts to get justice and eventually she wore down the judge's resolve and he gave her what she wanted. Even though this particular judge had no regard for justice, the widow's persistence won through. According to Jesus, if persistence can force even a corrupt judge to act, then it is all the more likely to prompt our just Heavenly Father to vindicate His children.

This is why it is so important that we persist in our asking. We mustn't give up when we think that nothing is happening. If we pray persistently, our Father will hear us and act.

Hold on to the substance of your faith

Faith is the substance of things hoped for and this is what we grasp and take hold of in prayer. This "substance" is the firm reality and clear conviction that our prayers are being heard. Once you know you have taken hold of something tangibly in prayer, never let it go! When we have the substance, the answer is as good as ours.

In our most difficult moments, when our faith is being stretched and tested to the limit, we are often tempted to throw away our confidence and let go of the conviction we had in prayer. But the truth that God is as good as His Word is what will give us the supernatural persistence we need. Hang on to this truth – it will sustain you through even the worst episodes of your life. The writer of Hebrews encourages us,

"Let us hold fast the confession of our hope without wavering, for He who promised is faithful."
(Hebrews 10:23)

God is always faithful to us and this is why we should and can persevere. God will never let us down and our confidence in Him will be rewarded.

Persistence prepares you for blessing

Persistence in prayer should ignite hope in us because it points to answers and leads the way to blessing. Through the act of persistence, God is preparing us to receive. Often God has to do something in us, before He gives something to us. He knows that prematurely answering our prayers could do us more harm than good and He does not allow that to happen. Every parent knows that it is necessary to discipline children by not always giving them what they want immediately. If we treated our children like this they would quickly become spoilt. That's why God says,

"You may have need of endurance, so that after you have done the will of God, you may receive the promise."

(Hebrews 10:36)

God is all-wise and all-loving and He wants to see godly character developed in us. So we must accept the disciplines of waiting, testing and persisting, because in time they will shape us in the Christlike people that God wants us to be.

Summary:

◊ Prayer need not be more complicated than just asking, but Jesus taught us also to be persistent and not give up. Sometimes we will pray and immediately receive our answer by faith, but at other times we are called on to pray persistently until we receive a breakthrough.

◊ In our most difficult times, it is very tempting to give up and stop persisting in prayer, but we have to learn to hold on. Often our answer is delayed because God needs to work to shape our character and prepare us to receive our answer. A premature answer may harm rather than bless us. God is faithful and we need to trust Him because He knows what He is doing. When we are called to persist in prayer this should make us glad because it points the way to our answer and our blessing.

18 *Praying with Thanksgiving*

As we approach the end of this book, I hope that you will take one truth deep into your spirit. I've repeated it throughout: prayer on its own doesn't get answers – it must be combined with something else. We have learned that we can mix prayer with,

◊ Confidence
◊ God's will
◊ Faith
◊ Confession
◊ Forgiveness
◊ Giving
◊ Fasting
◊ Action
◊ Persistence

There remains just one last ingredient: thanksgiving. God desires that our prayers to Him are seasoned with much praise and thankfulness. As the Psalmist writes simply and profoundly in Psalm 106:12,

"They believed His words; they sang His praise."

Throughout the Bible we see praise and thanksgiving used as a weapon. The truth is, it can be a powerful tool in times of trial and hardship. Through the darkest of times God's people have used praise and thanksgiving as a means of releasing the power of God. When Paul and Silas were in prison, they praised God together with all their might. This was not an attempt to get Him to act on their behalf – they simply praised God because He was worth praising – but He heard them nevertheless and sent an earthquake at midnight which released them from their chains.

In Paul and Silas' eyes, their difficult circumstances didn't reduce the amount of praise that God was worthy of receiving. Since heartfelt praise honours God, this actually prepares the way for Him to act.

"Whoever offers praise glorifies Me; and to him who orders his conduct aright I will show the salvation of God." (Psalm 50:23)

The Bible teaches us that God *inhabits* the praises of His people. If we are constantly filling our mouths with praise to God, then we are continuously benefiting from His presence.

Praise prepares the way for victory

The sound of our praises is a terrible noise in the ears of the enemy. Our praise has the effect of silencing our enemies. This is why we must learn to praise God at all times – before the battle, during the battle, and after the battle. Psalm 8:2 says,

"Out of the mouth of babes and infants You have ordained strength, because of Your enemies, that You may silence the enemy and the avenger."

Satan wants to silence our praise because it silences him! He has nothing to say in the presence of praise. Our praise reminds him of the greatness and goodness of God.

Pray with thanksgiving

Praise is a verbal declaration of the goodness of God, and God is good all the time. Praising God is a public proclamation of His virtues. But thanksgiving goes even further.

Each time we thank God, we speak directly to Him. Our thanksgiving is our *personal expression of gratitude* for what He has done for us. God wants thanksgiving to be mixed constantly with our prayers.

> *"Be anxious for nothing, but in everything by prayer and supplication, with thanksgiving, let your requests be made known to God."*   (Philippians 4:6)

And again we read,

> *"Rejoice always, pray without ceasing, in everything give thanks; for this is the will of God in Christ Jesus for you."*   (1 Thessalonians 5:16-18)

We empower our praying when we begin to mix asking with thanksgiving. Thanksgiving transports us away from need-based prayer and into the realm of faith. Thanksgiving helps us to concentrate more on God's resources and less on our circumstances. It draws our mind towards God's answers and away from our problems.

Whenever we want to thank someone who has done something special for us, we usually show our appreciation tangibly with a gift or a token of our appreciation. This is just as welcome to God as it is to us. The people of Israel understood this principle because their Law made special provision for thank offerings. These were sacrifices that God's people offered to Him as a way of showing their gratefulness.

"Offer to God thanksgiving, and pay your vows to the Most High. Call upon Me in the day of trouble; I will deliver you, and you shall glorify Me."
(Psalm 50:14-15)

Thank offerings were sometimes made to fulfil a vow. They were one of the ways in which the people of God could call upon the Lord in times of trouble and God promised to deliver them.

The Psalmist asks the question,

"What shall I render to the Lord for all His benefits toward me?"
(Psalm 116:12)

Then he provides the answer:

"I will offer to You the sacrifice of thanksgiving, and will call upon the name of the Lord. I will pay my vows to the Lord now in the presence of all his people."
(Psalm 116:17-18)

It's little wonder that he then cries,

"Oh, that men would give thanks to the Lord for His goodness, and for His wonderful works to the

children of men! Let them sacrifice the sacrifices of thanksgiving, and declare His works with rejoicing."
(Psalm 107:21-22)

Start mixing your prayers with....

Throughout this book I have endeavoured to faithfully explain how we can better cooperate with God in order to make our prayer lives more effective. I have seen these principles work over and over again in my own life and the lives of many other believers. I pray that you too are deep into the journey of discovering that prayer is life's greatest adventure.

I also pray that you will know God's great power working in your life through prayer and that you will learn to rejoice at all times in the wonderful goodness of God. For He is good indeed.

Summary:

◊ As well as combining our prayers with the other elements we have discussed, we need to mix prayer with thanksgiving. God desires our prayers to be laced with praise and gratitude.

◊ Through the Bible we can see praise and thanksgiving being used as a weapon. When expressed from pure motives, thanksgiving spoken out in difficult circumstances often preceded a spiritual breakthrough. God is moved to respond to our gratitude by pouring further blessing upon us. In this way, praise prepares the way for victory.

◊ God deserves our praise and thanksgiving because He is good and worthy of our praise. We can be constantly thankful because God's goodness towards us is constant and never-changing.